iWrite

Using Blogs, Wikis, and Digital Stories
in the English Classroom

Dana J. Wilber

HEINEMANN
Portsmouth, NH

Heinemann
361 Hanover Street
Portsmouth, NH 03801–3912
www.heinemann.com

Offices and agents throughout the world

Library of Congress Cataloging-in-Publication Data
Wilber, Dana J.
    iWrite : Using blogs, wikis, and digital stories in the English classroom / Dana J. Wilber.
        p. cm.
    Includes bibliographical references and index.
    ISBN-13: 978-0-325-01397-8
    ISBN-10: 0-325-01397-7
    1. English language—Study and teaching (Secondary)—Computer-assisted instruction. 2. Educational technology—United States.   I. Title.

LB1631.W392 2010
428.0078'5—dc22   2009040113

Editor: Cheryl Kimball
Production: Vicki Kasabian
Cover design: Geoff Bloom
Typesetter: Tom Allen, Pear Graphic Design
Manufacturing: Steve Bernier

Printed in the United States of America on acid-free paper
14 13 12 11 10   ML   1 2 3 4 5

To Chris, who understood all the hours I spent typing away
And to my grandfather, who always asked how the book was going

Contents

Acknowledgments

In this book, I tell stories of my own teaching at Montclair State University through the PreCollege Reading Program as well as my work done through the Improving Teacher Quality Program grant. I would like to express my thanks to, and deep respect for, my students in the PCRP classes and the teachers we worked with through the ITQP grant in East Orange, New Jersey. I have learned—and continue to learn—an enormous amount through this work. Thank you—for your time, for your stories, and for access to your classrooms and your lives.

I would also like to thank my colleagues Dr. Michele Knobel, Dr. Tina Jacobowitz, and Dr. Tamara Spencer, without whose support and cheering on this book never would have been completed. And enormous thanks to my research assistant, Sarah Davis, for her keen editing eye, quick hand at appendices, and ability to learn the *Chicago Manual of Style* overnight.

My heartfelt thanks to Jim Strickland at Heinemann for supporting this book. I can't even explain how excited I was to get that email—and from a leading person in the field, no less. His help was invaluable. Too, thanks go to Cheryl Kimball, whose close editing and excellent ideas made this a much better book.

Introduction
It's a Brave New World

Every day, when I walk from my car to my office on campus, I see students all around me immersed in technology. Many are using their cell phones, not to talk but to text each other—typing furiously as they wend through the crowd (and amazing me that they can do both at the same time). Others rush past, telltale white cords dangling from their ears as they listen to a hidden iPod or MP3 player.

Most of the students in the study lounges I pass are working on their laptops. Since our campus is wireless, they are doing anything from coursework to checking their Facebook page. Like any other campus in the United States, the majority of our students have a Facebook page and use it to communicate everything from their relationship status to their favorite books. They comment on each other's pages; some even seek out the few faculty on the site (I have a page) and add us as "friends." This is what it means to be a college student today. And what is really interesting is that I see many of the same behaviors at the middle and high schools down the road, perhaps with the exception of using laptops on a wireless network. From sixth to twelfth grades, students are texting, chatting, networking, and writing all over the place.

This book seeks to merge two important areas for teachers today: literacy and technology. As the world changes around us, we all become more and more aware of the ways in which we read and write or are called to communicate a message—and the technologies we have at our disposal in order to send those messages. This is true also of our students who, whether in middle school or college, read and write an extraordinary amount outside of school: on blogs, on personal pages on Facebook and MySpace, via texting and chat, or even through fan fiction based on favorite pop culture characters. It's not that our students aren't reading and writing, but where and what they are reading and writing is off the school radar, for the most part—at least until one genre, say instant messaging or texting, moves into another, like a school paper. We've all had students turn in papers with technologically derived abbreviations like IMHO (in my humble opinion) or gr8 (great). Our students, across the spectrum, need to be able to read and write more proficiently in academic genres just as they need to understand and view their participation online a bit more critically.

Often seen from two extremes—a magic bullet or an unnecessary tangle—technologies are simply tools that allow us to live our lives, more simply or in ways that deepen them, depending on how we use these tools. Technologies, in and of themselves, are not necessarily bad or good. They are the tools we choose to use as a part of our lives in myriad ways. As a result, more and more, the lives of teenagers are mediated and moderated by technologies that were new less than ten years ago. As their lives are lived more and more online, however, the boundaries between public and private begin to blur and our students struggle to understand the repercussions.

At the base of this struggle is a need to understand genre and audience in the midst of what is an ongoing technological revolution. At no point, however, do I mean to advocate for technologies over the reading and writing instruction that happens in your classroom. Because the tools have changed, our students need to be ever-more savvy about which tools they choose and the repercussions of each. And we need to know more about the technologies that shape the ways our students read and write in their everyday lives. Our students choose from email, text messaging, instant messaging, blogs, Facebook/MySpace and other social networks, Twitter, social bookmarking, Google Earth, digital storytelling, and more to communicate daily. Not everything they do belongs in the classroom. But it makes sense for us, as teachers, to know about these technologies since they occupy so much of our students' lives and because they are a big part of the ways in which students read and write today. And some new technologies lend themselves well to teaching reading and writing in the literacy classroom. This book concerns three tools that are easy to use and have free websites and instructions to help you get started.

Blogs, wikis, and digital stories are good tools to start with because of their ease in use, free application in many cases, and versatility. Simply defined, a *blog* (shortened from "weblog") is a website that is written by one person or a group of people with posts listed in reverse chronological order—the newest first—and is an easy way to publish to the Web. A wiki, on the other hand, is a website that acts as a resource for information that can be collaboratively edited. Both can be either public or private, depending on how you choose to set them up and apply them, and both can be accessed by anyone with a Web connection. They can incorporate written text, visual images, audio, and video. A digital story is a narrative that begins with a storyboard or script and then is constructed of digital or computerized still images and/or video, together with audio including music and recorded voice. Digital stories can be fiction, non-fiction, or a combination of the two. All three of these technologies allow users to write electronic texts that can be published online and used to gather resources, create classroom blogs and communities, and much more. Throughout this book, I will show you how using these three tools can help support language arts learning with your students in your classroom and beyond.

Thomas Friedman, a columnist for the *New York Times*, writes that "the world is flat," meaning that everything today has become interconnected across the globe. As I will discuss more, we have moved into a world termed *Web 2.0*; that is, dependent on the creation, collaboration, and diffusion of ideas and messages (Lankshear and Knobel 2006). What it means to read and write is changing quickly, even before our students can take into account different genres and texts when creating or receiving a message. Our teenagers have access to such a wide variety of ways for making meaning that teaching students how to discern between media is a tough charge, but an essential one.

For example, what and how teens communicate on Instant Messenger should be different from how they write for their classes, and even from the email messages they send (particularly to adults or for more formal reasons). Issues of genre, audience, voice, and style are the natural domain of the English classroom and if we take on the multiple forms of student reading and writing outside of class, we naturally begin to work with reading and writing that are authentic and motivating to our students. Now I want to be very clear—I don't mean that we should necessarily have our students create MySpace pages for class, for example. Some practices belong to our students; it makes no sense educationally or otherwise to bring every technology students use into the literacy classroom.

Yet there are many technologies beyond word processing that can be used to support and encourage student literacy, especially in a workshop setting. These technologies, including blogs, wikis, Google applications, fan fiction, filmmaking, and digital video projects, can be used to scaffold our students as they find their voice and learn how to communicate in a world constituted by millions of authors.

Using collaborative technologies in the literacy classroom builds on the ease with which teenagers pick up lingo and expertise around certain types of technology use, like creating a page on MySpace or even posting a video to YouTube, while at the same time addressing their struggle with doing some academic tasks like researching effectively online—finding the right sources, comprehending the information they do find, and avoiding plagiarism. Many think of this generation, often named the "Millennial Generation" (Howe and Strauss 2000), as being automatically expert in and comfortable with new technologies, especially as compared with their teachers and parents. Prensky (2001) terms this a divide between "digital natives," those students who grew up in a world shaped by the Internet and its associated technologies, and "digital immigrants," those of us who remember a world before cell phones, CDs, the World Wide Web, and even email.

Yet in my experience, a single divide between expert teenagers and less expert teachers isn't that simple. Sure, there are many things our students know how to do online that we don't—but they don't know everything. In particular, they often have not thought through the differences between public and private spaces, or legitimate and false sources—even though they use the Internet to publish or research an enormous variety of texts. What does seem clear is that the use of technology is incredibly motivating and important to students who believe that their knowledge of these new technologies is key to their survival long after their schooling has ended. And they're probably right.

Chapter 1 describes the lives of Millennials and the new technologies that are embedded into their everyday ways of using reading and writing to make sense of the world. Chapter 2 goes on to explain how, when new technologies interact with reading and writing, new practices or new literacies develop that can be used in your classroom. Chapters 3 and 4 explain in more detail—with examples from all over the World Wide Web—what blogs, wikis, and digital stories are, and provide you with instructions as to how to set up and use these tools. Chapter 5 goes further to show how wikis, blogs, and digital stories can be used to address ten key issues in the literacy classroom; Chapter 6 gives a brief overview of new technologies that are on the horizon, in order to familiarize you with the newest tools you might use someday soon.

My hope is that, with this book, you come to see some of the ways that new technologies have given students opportunities to read and write in powerful ways every day. Even with all of the dire predictions about kids not reading or writing today, we know that they spend a lot of time online and that being online involves reading and writing. We can build a bridge between the literate lives of our students outside of school and the literacies we want to teach them in our classrooms by capitalizing on their expertise, interest, and engagement with new technologies.

What It Means to Teach Reading and Writing Today

Vinnie* sat in my class for an entire semester and never uttered a word unless I asked him a direct question. He kept his New York Yankees cap pulled low over his face and slouched down so far in his chair that at times the bill of the cap almost touched his desk. More than once, I caught him asleep, his chin nodding just above his chest.

Vinnie's assignments, when he did them, were terse and surface level; I couldn't really get a handle on what he knew and what he didn't. If I called on him in class, he became red and even quieter, and a painful silence descended as we waited either for Vinnie to speak or for me to give up and call on someone else. No matter what I did, I didn't feel like I knew Vinnie at all. At the end of the semester, he was just as much a mystery to me as he was at the beginning. After all the weeks he spent in my class, I felt like I had barely gotten through to him; I wasn't sure Vinnie knew much more or thought much differently on the last day than he had on the first.

I wish I could say Vinnie was an anomaly but, unfortunately, he wasn't. I teach a basic literacy class, required for students whose incoming scores

---

*Student names have been changed.

demonstrate a need to work on their reading, writing, and thinking in order to be successful in college. These are the students most at risk of dropping out, and from the very beginning of their college careers, they're angry and ashamed that they have to take a reading class at all. Something in their preparation didn't go quite right; for many reasons, these students graduated high school unable to meet college literacy demands.

On occasion, I got it right—achieving the necessary balance between teaching students and helping them learn on their own. Sometimes they got excited about the class; sometimes I found the right books for them, and they made the connection between who they are as readers and writers and how successful they could be. But the successes seemed few and far between. Using traditional reading assignments and occasional papers typically left my students frustrated and me wondering what to do differently. What I decided to do differently was to implement blogging—and things began to change.

How It All Started

As a young professor and former seventh-grade teacher, I had taught literacy methods courses for several years, both to kids and to preservice teachers. I had never taught a basic skills or remedial class before, however. I started my teaching career in an urban, seventh-grade, balanced literacy course, but since that time, I had come to work nearly exclusively with preservice and inservice teachers through professional workshops and college teaching. In other words, I was used to teaching *how* to teach literacy effectively, but it had been a while since I had taught literacy itself.

I came into the classroom with the misconception that college students would be excited to take the course and ready to learn whatever I offered. I was wrong. These students were frustrated and confused about being labeled as deficient at the college level, just as students are in high school and middle school. (Several didn't know there was such a thing as a reading class for college students.) Many had good GPAs, but had made it all the way through high school without ever learning to be truly effective writers and readers. In particular, they struggled with using writing in order to demonstrate what they knew; these students were not comfortable with writing in order to explain, and were even less comfortable with themselves as writers. These students could think of a hundred things they would rather do than read a book, write a letter, or discuss literature—all typical literacy tasks in a middle or high school English class. And they were forced to take this class in their first year in order to continue college. I realized that my college-age basic literacy students weren't so different from my seventh graders after all.

So I turned back to my training as a middle school balanced literacy teacher and tried to implement the workshop model in the classroom, as well as a reader-response-based approach to reading. My idea was that using a work-shop model for writing and a response method for reading would build on students' interests and keep them motivated as they learned. So I asked students to work through drafts of their writing, had them respond to the things we read, and tried to come up with writing prompts and reading assignments suited to their interests and experiences. At first, I just focused on the reading and writing aspects of the class—teaching academic literacy by assigning research papers, reading assignments, and traditional comprehension tasks. I stayed within the traditional boundaries of a college reading course, using a text that focused on skill development, asking students to read and complete comprehension tasks, teaching basic research skills, and assigning a research paper.

Most of the writing my students turned in, however, was pretty flat—papers that were essentially empty except for restating ideas we went over in class discussions. The echo was overwhelming; I felt like they were just telling me what I wanted to hear. One after another, as they brought up their drafts for me to look at or raised their hands in class, they would ask, "Is this right?" "Is this what I should do?" "Is this what you want?" Hardly any of them trusted their own voice, and none pushed back even enough to ask why we were doing the things we were doing. If the university told them they needed to take a reading class, they were going to do just what I asked of them—noth-ing more, and often less. After all, what did I, as an Ivy League graduate, know about having a hard time reading, writing, and understanding?

As the semesters piled up and I taught the class over and over again, the same issues stood out. I didn't have daily contact with these students, as I had had with my seventh graders, but I got to see patterns that were emerging pretty clearly—and they weren't very different from the patterns my seventh graders showed when they struggled with comprehending. Twice a week my college students came in and sat quietly in their seats while I did most of the talking. I tried to get interesting discussions going about things I thought would spark their interest and connect to their lives, but to them, this was a reading and writing class period. What exactly did this have to do with real life, anyhow?

These were the same questions and concerns I saw teachers struggling with in middle and high school classes. Rarely did some of their students want to engage in academic reading and writing tasks. Instead, they read Spark-Notes and, inadvertently or not, copied from information they found online without really absorbing it. I wasn't the only one struggling to connect with these students—far from it. It took me a little time, but I suddenly realized that the connection was staring me in the face: I watched as students all across campus listened to their iPods while furiously text messaging on their cell phones.

Literacy in Students' Lives Today

Let's go back to Vinnie for a second. Born and raised nearby, he had always planned to go to college even though he wasn't entirely sure what he wanted to do when he got there. The things he loved to do weren't related to school—playing video games, watching movies, and spending time at the beach. He was pretty good with cars and an avid football fan, spending time at as many NFL games in the area as he could.

When I asked him at the beginning of the semester what he had been reading lately, Vinnie couldn't remember the last time he had picked up a book; he wasn't sure he had ever finished one, even if it had been assigned for school. As for writing, he hated it more than anything else and struggled with every word he put down on the page. Vinnie was never sure what the teacher wanted or why some of the things he wrote were judged wrong; he had no sense of why writing and reading might be important in his life, other than because he had to do schoolwork to be successful. Along with my class, Vinnie was struggling to make it through College Writing I, which was also taught using a workshop model with multiple drafts, peer editing, and conferencing with the teacher. Despite all of this support, Vinnie had not earned higher than a C on his essays through the semester thus far.

Yet Vinnie wasn't illiterate in the least. He read many things regularly—from emails to several sports websites and the sports page of more than one newspaper. He also wrote countless emails and text messages throughout the course of a day, authored his own MySpace page, and commented on videos posted to YouTube as well as on a football fan site. He could and did conduct research regularly online both for school and to find out about things he was interested in, using key words and trying to discern the best sources, although not always successfully. He could make sense of computer game and car manuals, as well as the densest baseball or football statistics page. Although he wrote and read regularly outside of school, school reading and writing turned him off. To Vinnie, the literacies required in school were hoops he had to jump through on his way to a career and (he hoped) a good life.

Vinnie was far from alone in his thinking. There was also Shin. A recent immigrant from Korea, Shin was in her first semester of college in the United States, and only her third semester as a student in an American system. Already somewhat quiet, Shin struggled to express even simple thoughts in English; her parents and grandmother spoke Korean, and Shin's younger brother was the only other English speaker in the house. Sometimes Shin would have to miss school to translate for her parents, standing with them in the lines at the driver's license bureau or helping fill out and file visa paperwork. These interruptions in her schedule put her English and academic development in the United States further behind.

Shin was far from lacking intelligence; she had been an excellent student in Korea, a fluent reader and confident writer. But coming to the United States and learning English as a high school junior had been extremely difficult. English as a Second Language (ESL) classes in her urban high school had not helped much. Shin worked hard on her assignments, but her writing was incoherent, rambling, and difficult to follow because of her unfamiliarity with American English syntax. Sympathetic teachers passed Shin on semester after semester, and her writing remained undeveloped, primarily because she didn't have to write very often. Most of her reading and writing classes in high school had required very little work, and her English language learner (ELL) status excused her from the most strenuous assessments. She had no idea how she was going to be successful at a college taught in English.

Shin maintained her literacy and fluency in Korean, however, by speaking, reading, and writing the language throughout her daily life. Her family, friends, and church community were all Korean; English was rarely used in most of the places she went outside of school. Shin preferred to read in Korean, and she sent many emails in Korean to friends back home. She was also a member of a social networking site—like MySpace but specifically for Korean teenagers and primarily written in Korean (with some English). It would have taken a professor fluent in Korean to discover exactly what Shin understood and could do in the classroom, given her limited English.

James was another example of a dissociated student. A football player for the school, he struggled with balancing his course load with a heavy practice schedule. He was constantly exhausted in class, and sometimes missed sessions because he was sleeping or working out. James wasn't sure what to prioritize—he knew school was important, but he wasn't very successful at it, whereas on the football field, James was a star.

One of the things that were hardest for James was asking for help and explaining what he didn't understand, especially in reading and writing. While his teachers seemed to expect him to figure out where he had gotten lost, James spent most of the class time genially nodding along with the lecture, confused but unable to pinpoint the place where his understanding had broken down. His class papers were rambling and off topic because he had difficulty understanding the assignments and producing cohesive products, even though he was often interested in the topics and wanted to improve.

Neena, on the other hand, usually understood quite well what was going on in class. She felt, though, like her professors and peers couldn't care less what she had to think or say regarding any of the topics. A commuter student, Neena spent nearly as much time looking for a parking space as she actually did in class. She lived at home because of financial constraints, and since she was home, she often got stuck babysitting or taking care of other family responsibilities.

Instead of being immersed in the college experience, Neena felt disconnected from the campus, classes, and community. Taking a remedial reading class just made it worse and made her feel like she was wasting money she didn't have for a class that wouldn't count. She knew how to read: after all, she was the first member of her family to go to college and had always been considered smart and outspoken. But her strong personality and interest in connecting her own experiences of growing up in an urban environment to what she was learning often seemed unwelcome in classes where, most of the time, the teacher talked at the students instead of with them.

Both Neena and James used writing outside of class almost incessantly via technology—emailing and text messaging friends and family to stay in contact. In fact, Neena's Sidekick (a cell phone designed to make text messaging easier, it has a horizontal orientation and a full keyboard) was her most prized possession. She preferred to use the keyboard to communicate, rather than the phone component, and could carry on multiple text conversations at the same time while listening to music. James and Neena were each avid members of both MySpace and Facebook, and spent countless hours updating their pages and adding friends.

Neena, Vinnie, James, and Shin were, at some point, middle schoolers and high schoolers. Their counterparts can be found in a freshman World Literature class, junior English class, or middle school language arts class. Across the spectrum, students struggle with their abilities to make meaning using literacy—whether reading, writing, speaking, or thinking. My first-year college students were hardly anomalies—like many students, they were interested in the world and in being successful, but they lacked some of the skills for achieving that success. More important, students like Vinnie and the others didn't see themselves as literate individuals at all, not as "readers" or "writers," for the most part. Yet these are the very students we are trying to reach. The more sophisticated writing and reading we can ask of them now, in schools, will better prepare them for the workplace, where emphasis will be placed on their literacy skills and interests.

And these students aren't alone. According to recent research, 70 percent of students in grades 4 through 12 are low-achieving writers (Persky, Daane, and Jin 2003). More than 7,000 students drop out of high school each day, and those at the most risk for dropping out are at the lowest literacy levels (Biancarosa and Snow 2006). According to the most recent National Assessment of Educational Progress, or NAEP, in 2002, 69 percent of eighth-grade students and 77 percent of twelfth-grade students did not meet proficiency goals in writing. More and more companies and schools are expressing dismay at the writing abilities of recent hires, even to the point of having to offer training courses in writing correct reports, emails, and analyses (Hart 2005). The same kinds of statistics hold true for reading. The literacy skills of our students aren't matching up to what they need to be as they progress on to high school, college, and the workforce. But these students aren't unintelligent, and they have developed expertise in a world that has largely come about in a very short time—a world so different from that of traditional education that it seems almost completely opposed to it. As educators, it is vitally important to know the world they inhabit.

The Millennials

Millennials, according to Howe and Strauss, are those students born after 1982 (this date cutoff means that the students were eighteen or younger at the turn of the century). My freshmen this semester were born in 1989 or 1990. Before many of them could read, the Internet came on the scene. They don't remember a world before cell phones, email, and the World Wide Web. They grew up chatting on AOL and creating pages and blogs on MySpace and LiveJournal. Additionally, they do almost all their homework online while simultaneously listening to music, chatting with friends via computer, and completing other tasks.

According to the Digital Youth Project Report from the MacArthur Foundation Report on Living and Learning with Digital Media (Ito et al. 2008), the lives of teenagers are marked by the presence of "always-on communication"—teens are always connected to one another through multiple media and for multiple reasons, including friendship, romance, school, and other purposes. These relationships are mediated on- and offline—a distinction that teens often do not see to the degree that adults do. Teens will continue relationships with the best media at their disposal for the purpose at hand, according to Palfrey and Gasser (2008) in their book *Born Digital: Understanding the First Generation of Digital Natives*.

The lives of adolescents are so marked by new technologies that teens use multiple modes of communication to stay constantly connected, play with forming and reforming a new sense of identity through participation in online social networking sites like MySpace and Facebook, and move almost seamlessly between privately and publicly mediated communication—from texting to chatting to posting on semipublic and public sites. For our students, the definitions of friendship, communication, dating, flirting, community, self, identity, connection, media, hanging out, and more are mediated by on- and offline technologies, often in ways we are just beginning to understand.

Too, new media like online texts and new technologies like email and the Internet are deeply embedded in the ways in which our students go about learning, thinking, reading, and writing. Our students turn automatically to technology to do research, find out about a book, define a word, write a paper or a poem, and a multitude of other tasks. Nearly everything they do is mediated by these technologies, the likes of which we could hardly have conceived of just ten years ago. These students are the ultimate multitaskers, but they often have difficulty completing tasks and aren't always clear about the boundaries between cutting and pasting quotes and plagiarism, for example. They are extremely likely to look directly to technology to help them with their homework and solve their problems—from reading books online through the use of SparkNotes to discussing math problems through Instant Messenger with a friend or doing research by looking up sites online.

These activities mean that our students learn and interact differently with texts than we did or than our parents did. For example, what we consider traditional plagiarism is a simple act of cut and paste to these students, making plagiarism and problems with attribution of sources that much more complex. They need to begin to understand that this does constitute the theft of ideas, regardless of the ease with which they can get the information. Bringing in page upon page printed from the Web as their "research" for a research paper is not the same as doing research unless they have read and analyzed what they found. Often, Millennial students focus on getting the information when we would like them to shift their attention to understanding, synthesizing, and analyzing that information. In addition, our students may not understand the difference between information posted on a blog, regardless of the author, and that found on a site like the *New York Times*, *Encyclopedia Britannica*, or even Wikipedia (I discuss Wikipedia in more detail throughout this book).

Millennials are surrounded by new technologies that they use constantly and that have come to shape their reading and writing. All these tools have what are thought of as new affordances; that is, they allow us to do new things with reading and writing—such as texting, which gives us new ways to use language—and those affordances shape how we come to see language and literacy over time. In addition, we need to understand these different ways our students work today. One of the major differences is their connectivity.

Our students are used to an instantaneous and ongoing connection to others; they have had this kind of communication since they can remember. Whether via cell phone (voice and texting), instant messaging, email, video chat, blogging, or social networks, no one is alone for long. Our students draw on this connectivity to learn, socialize, and survive—so it is understandable that they would want to do the same when completing class work. A problem arises when a teacher expects student work to be individual, at least until a draft is complete and ready to be edited, and students are discussing and even working together on assignments. In a case study I conducted in 2002, my student would often discuss her assignments with her friends on IM, all the while doing online research (and watching television, chatting on her cell, and searching for videos of the swim team online). This is certainly different from the "ideal" study or writing context, and yet this is very much the world of our students. The question then becomes: What strategies can we teach our students so they can help one another while still preserving the individual integrity of their work? And how does working this way change the nature of reading and writing?

Another issue of the Millennials is the simultaneity I just described. We may have been taught that the best way to get work done was alone, with perhaps only music in the background. That is not the way most of our students work, however. Their attention is divided as they multitask, a manner of working that may or may not be successful. Recent research suggests that multitasking is not really possible, but results in doing just short, sequential tasks (Tugend 2008). So the question of how to divide attention efficiently and successfully is a key one for students.

One example illustrates this. When students are asked to read and write about classic literature, many begin and end with the SparkNotes version of the text, rather than the book itself. More detailed even than Cliffs Notes, SparkNotes provides scene or chapter-by-chapter summaries for free that are downloadable. Sections for each book illustrate themes, key points, important questions explained, and more. The question many of our students naturally ask is, Why read the entire book? Isn't the most important stuff available online? What does a traditional book (and written response to that book) have that SparkNotes hasn't covered? We need to have answers to that question—to help students understand that their interpretation and written response to literature, for example, is unique. In an era of easy answers and constant exposure to information, our students need to develop an individual critical eye and voice in order to stand out from the crowd. They may do this by using unusual tools, such as online chatting with friends about the book, but they also need to read the traditional texts.

So teachers of writing (as well as of other subjects and texts) need to help their students understand how to bridge resources like SparkNotes and the actual texts they will need to know well by the time they enter college. We have to teach writing in a way that makes use of the new tools that effectively scaffold writing, and yet not adopt every kind of technology just because it exists. We need to update the reading and writing process model to incorporate useful technologies. And, perhaps most important, we need to become familiar with these tools ourselves.

Why Are Reading and Writing Even More Important Today?

Even as we move into a digital age, the written word may become more, not less, important. We and our students are bombarded with information and messages from the time we wake up and log on to check our email messages or turn on our phones to check text messages, to the last message we send before we fall asleep. We read the news online, send messages to family and friends, and post to sites like MySpace. We watch clips from television and movies on sites like Facebook and comment on them. Some of us keep blogs already, writing about our thoughts, experiences, or the things we find online. Newspaper readership has moved online in many cases, and paper subscriptions drop. Much of the research we do is online; we use the phrase "to google" interchangeably with "looking something up"—and it's even styled with a lowercase *g*. The Internet, cell phones, instant messaging, electronic mapping, digital video and cameras, and many more technologies are deeply intertwined with our lives. Imagine losing your cell phone for twenty-four hours. Not only would you lose a medium for communication, but you would probably lose contact information for those closest to you. You might lose days' or months' worth of text messages with important information like addresses, appointments, or cell numbers. Some of us would lose email messages stored on our phones or GPS information with locations of places where we need to be. Almost all of us would lose pictures that were probably not backed up to anything else. And this is just your phone, a single technology you use to communicate and connect each day.

What does literacy have to do with cell phones? Simply put, we use language, including written text and visual imagery, to use our phones. In fact, we use language with just about every digital technology we have. As these technologies change and evolve, the ways in which we use language do as well. Schools and teachers must come to understand these changes and the impact they have on students, schools, and societies if we want to teach our students in the best ways possible.

Learning, Being, Connecting: Creating, Innovating, Remixing

Literacy today involves digital technologies from cell phones to the Internet, from personal pages on sites like Facebook to online versions of books and newspapers. Video, pictures, poems, books, signs, songs, and much more are communicated digitally, and all involve language—whether visual, as in the making and communicating of visual images and signs, or written, as in books, poems, and news stories. We began using the Web for information gathering, but today, in 2010, digital technologies are embedded in our lives to such a degree that learning, being, and connecting are all mediated by them.

In terms of learning, much of the information that we gather, let alone that which comes to us each day, is delivered digitally. We have to somehow find the sources of all the information we get, seek out the valid ones, and determine what to do with the information. Our learning is conveyed by these technologies; for us and for our students, computers and the Internet are generally the first places to which we turn when we want to learn about something. What are the repercussions of this? How do we teach students to learn using

Google, search terms, and online search engines rather than dictionaries and the Dewey Decimal System? How do we learn by delving into and fighting our way through the thicket of information available to us, literally around the clock? And what does it mean to learn when the information immediately presents itself, with little clue as to its significance when compared with other information? The very ease with which we can gather so much often belies the importance of what we find.

In the same manner, we can easily use the Internet and digital technologies to represent ourselves to the world. Beyond sending email and text messages, we can become members of social networking sites like Facebook and MySpace (more on this later) and describe ourselves, posting information about our likes and dislikes and connecting to other people, some of whom we haven't seen in years. We can post comments on other people's pages through videos on YouTube and on news stories. We can create pages to represent ourselves, have our own blogs, and write websites for our class. We can make a mark on the world such that when we type our name into Google, results pop up that place us in the world. Digital technologies have come to shape our being, allowing us to present and re-present ourselves anew each day.

These technologies also shape the connections we have to one another, making tangible friendships and creating webs that link across physical spaces and even span the globe. These webs can extend the classroom beyond four walls and into learning spaces with other students around the world; they can bring resources in from all over that would be impossible to access otherwise. This kind of connecting through digital language—messaging, emailing, and posting to pages—has become central to our lives, and while it may not represent the kind of language we most want our students to use in the classroom, it does reveal the centrality of reading and writing digitally in their lives, a fact that is hard to dismiss. Learning, being, and connecting digitally are influenced by written, visual, and oral language used constantly by our students. We can't really say that they aren't reading and writing. They are. They just aren't reading and writing in the ways in which we might want them to, or in the ways schools encourage. My question is, What connections can we forge between their digital literacy and our academically traditional literacy?

One connection is to think more deeply about the ways in which students use language digitally. Yes, they write, read, and create text messages, instant messages, posts on each other's pages, comments on posts, videos, and comments on videos. All these practices involve the creation of a message. Instead of corralling information, students are actively involved in creating messages that must be written so that the receiver will understand them. Our students often are creating complex messages: digital videos with embedded texts, or abbreviations that make use of sophisticated wordplay and poetry as well as simplified messages, as researchers like David Crystal (2008) have found. It's easy to think of all digital messaging as throwaway writing, but it's not that simple. Abbreviations work only when they follow some sort of rule or pattern that both the author and reader can follow; for example, most text and IM abbreviations make use of phonics rules and cues.

Other messages that students create online include posts on personal pages, blogs, and even multimodal messages that include visual images, video, and music or other aural components. They are learning to create texts that are very different from the linear, written, paper-based texts that schools depend on, yet these online texts are central to a digital, information-based world and to their lives in ways that school assignments aren't. These new texts are motivating our students. They are connected to their sense of themselves, part of the social networks that populate their lives, and embedded in other texts in their world, such as movies, games, and even popular books like Harry Potter.

Thousands of stories have been posted on fan fiction sites like www.harrypotterfanfiction.com that retell the story of Harry Potter from other perspectives; these are texts that adolescents and adults have created just from love of the story and a desire to tell or retell it from another point of view. Through these sites, others read the stories and give the authors feedback—precisely the kinds of reading and writing behaviors we want to foster. Yet these stories aren't turned in as school assignments, but posted to public websites for anyone to read—done for the sheer joy of the topic and the chance to write themselves into a larger narrative.

Creating a message that can be seen by a larger audience, even potentially by anyone in the world, is a vital part of what it means for our students to be literate today. They can be creators in ways we couldn't when we were their age, and so the kinds of writing we ask them to do can seem limited by comparison. What does it mean to write a persuasive essay to turn in that only the teacher will read when they can write a persuasive post on their Facebook page that hundreds of friends will see? Or a research paper with a printed bibliography as compared to a blog post with direct links to research that supports points? Perhaps surprisingly, our students are interested in a wide range of topics and spend quite a bit of time online learning about them—fashion, the recent election, global warming, music, video games—and they are capable of creating sophisticated texts about them that make use of links, embedded video, and more. They know how to get these messages out to people as well, whether through MySpace or YouTube. Creation, innovation, and authorship are not new to our students, although they also should be able to think critically as well as creatively about the texts they create.

A practice that has come about in this digital age and that our students engage in has been termed *remixing* by Lawrence Lessig (2008), among others. Remixing involves taking someone else's creation—whether a written text, a work of art, a film, or a song—and making something new from it. Mostly, remixing has come to the public eye through questions of copyright, and as teachers we have to deal with the inevitable and essential issue of plagiarism. Thanks to digital technologies, our students have access to an unprecedented number of texts and works, and their abilities to create and innovate mean they can do a wide number of things with them. The question becomes, then, what is an innovation or creation and what is plagiarism? Can a student embed links to research rather than create a traditional bibliography? And does she or he understand that embedding links is different than cutting and pasting large sections of someone else's work into their own? The ease with which students can use others' work in creating their own doesn't mean they should, of course, but these issues need to be raised directly and specifically with them.

Literacy is changing, and teaching literacy must change along with it. Our students can create, innovate, and remix as they read and write in vastly different ways than we could. Chapter 3 discusses thinking about these new practices as new literacies and explains how to build on the experiences of students to bridge their technological expertise and the integration of technology into the literacy classroom. There is a lot we can do and much we can build on, but the blending is tricky. We have a great deal to teach our students and ourselves about what can and should be done with new technologies and how to teach literacy in a new millennium.

Why Do We Still Struggle with Teaching and Learning Literacy?

One of the problems may be that the literacy tasks required of students in school settings are or seem divorced from any real-world context. For many students, formal reading and writing are things done only at the demand of a teacher, rather than as valuable practices that enrich their lives. Many middle school, high school, and college students struggle with writing, postponing papers until the last minute or having a first draft serve as the final draft because they are unsure about editing and revising. Despite all our efforts, writing is still seen by most students as a skill you are either born with or you aren't, rather than as an ongoing practice that improves over time and with effort.

Yet students are reading and writing outside of school almost incessantly. While that might not seem to be the kind of reading and writing we would like them to do, there is something about the motivation, authenticity, and interest (among other things) that I think we as literacy teachers can build on.

> While the incessant reading and writing that children are doing outside school may not seem like the kind of reading and writing we would like them to do, there is something about the motivation, authenticity, and interest that I think we as literacy teachers can build on.

Starting a New Conversation

As mentioned before, the students described in this chapter are typical of many middle school, high school, and even college students. They struggle with academic tasks—in particular, reading and writing practices that foster deeper thinking and learning. Despite the implementation of the reading and writing workshop approach in many schools and classrooms, some of the same issues remain that were present in more traditional teaching styles. Too, the workshop approach is defined and applied differently by teachers in different settings, and each of us runs into our own problems in making it work in our classrooms. I would venture a guess that none of us teaching writing and reading are doing it perfectly—we all have issues, problems, and difficult students. This book is about reaching those students by building on what they love and do regularly without prodding—use and communicate via new technologies. Writing is writing, and teaching it well is difficult. While I have found that new technologies help in many ways, there are also "old school" ways to address these problems and concerns. Yet because new technologies are embedded into the lives of our students, these technologies are coming to shape their ideas of what it means to read, write, think, and learn. This is the beginning, as I see it, of a larger conversation about teaching literacy, continuing to improve what we do, and, most important, helping our students succeed in the twenty-first century.

We and our students struggle with literacy, often in terms of a disconnect between the kinds of reading and writing we ask them to do in school and the kinds of reading and writing they do outside of school. Specifically, our students have little practice in reading and writing for any length of time, for authentic purposes, in ways that seem relevant to their lives, in safe spaces that encourage them to take risks, and in ways that take into account that reading and writing are closely related to issues of personal identity. Thanks to mandated curricula and state assessments, it is hard to create opportunities to build on student interests and to create projects that allow for student inquiry, thereby increasing motivation. And in a world focused on product, assessment, and goals, the process and scope of cognitive development over time frequently get lost. We know the things that are or would be good for our students, but we're often caught in a larger system that makes it hard to provide those things for them. What if, however, we could use new, interactive technologies to provide some of those things?

So, Which Technologies Would Work?

The next chapter will go into specific technologies in much more detail, but it is my general position that including new technologies to support reading and writing just makes sense. Connecting to new technologies can build on what students know and can motivate students because being on the computer is something with which they are familiar and that often seems more authentic.

More and more teenagers are creating content to post online, according to research done by groups like the Pew Internet and American Life Project and the MacArthur Digital Youth Project, and the move toward content creation suggests a kind of authorship with which are students are familiar. Some of the tools they use are good connections for us, as teachers, to build on. There are too many new technologies and tools to discuss all of them in a book of this nature, so I focus on the tools that seem best suited to creating authentic opportunities to respond to reading, to writing better and more clearly, and to learning about a variety of modes for making meaning—in short, tools that relate directly to the issues we face today in teaching literacy. Those tools are: blogs or weblogs, wikis, and digital storytelling. All have a particular grammar, or way of expressing meaning; all require a metacognitive understanding of how to create that meaning; and all can work well in the classroom.

Blogs and wikis are digital technologies that are still mostly comprised of written text; both can use video and images and link to resources online, but students and teachers generally use blogs and wikis as easy resources to publish a wide array of text types to the Internet. This makes them a perfect middle step for a classroom trying to integrate a technology that still is centered around reading and writing and that uses free or inexpensive online tools. Students and teachers can easily learn blogs and wikis, they can be accessed from any computer with an Internet connection regardless of whether you have a Mac or PC, and both blogs and wikis allow you as a teacher to set different levels of privacy as you desire. As you will see throughout the book, blogs and wikis are also perfect scaffolds because you can move from teacher-centered versions to allow more student control and authorship as it becomes appropriate. As well, because blogs and wikis publish directly to the Web, parents, administrators, other members of the community, and even other teachers and schools all over the world can make use of your expertise.

So, why digital stories? Like blogs and wikis, digital stories are natural tools for the literacy classroom. While they are more visual in the form of the final project, the steps involved in creating a digital story—including research, storyboarding, scripting, and interviewing—all involve heavy reading and writing. Digital stories are particularly motivating for students who struggle with reading and writing because of their visual component, and they serve as excellent opportunities for group work and collaboration. They are a natural next step after blogging and using wikis for students who want to create digital texts, particularly as a summative assessment for a project.

Overall, while the range of tools and techniques that can be drawn on for the literacy classroom is vast, blogs, wikis, and digital stories are three technologies that can serve a range of needs, support both beginner and intermediate technology users, and motivate and build on student expertise, as I show in the rest of this book.

2 New Literacies for New Times

Why do new technologies work so well for so many students? Why are our kids so fascinated by new ways to connect, create, communicate? Is there any interest left in traditional modes of reading and writing? Has everything changed?

At this point, you may very well be wondering about the answers to these questions and more, particularly if the world of technology has the potential to change many of the ways you teach and how students are successful. New technologies seem integrated into all of our lives, and some of them, like cell phones, have become indispensable. Where a teacher of writing and literacy can become interested and begin to find answers is in the intersection of language, literacy, and new technologies. Not all technologies need to be used in all situations, nor should a writing teacher adopt only writing online through blogs, wikis, and other Web 2.0 technologies. But understanding why these kinds of technologies appeal to students and how we, as educators, can build on that appeal helps our students become better writers and even critical readers.

This chapter goes into much more than blogs, wikis, and digital stories in order to give you a sense of how new literacies work in the lives of our students before focusing, through the rest of the book, on how to use blogs, wikis, and digital stories. My reason for this is twofold: first, in order to understand how blogs, wikis, or digital storytelling can be used to develop student reading and writing in your classroom, it is important to learn a little bit more about how literacy is being impacted by new technologies. Second, through using blogs, wikis, and digital stories, you will probably come into contact with other, new technologies, and it is important that you have a basic understanding of how they work. All these new technologies are a part of the shift to Web 2.0 applications, where users can create content—an important change that becomes crucial to capitalize on in your own classroom through blogs, wikis, and digital stories. This chapter explains that shift in both literacy and digital technologies.

Literacy as Plural: To Be Literate Means Many Things

Most of us learned to think of literacy as the ability to read and write. But what we know now, through research and good practice, is that literacy really isn't as simple as "Vanessa is a good reader" or "Michael can really write." As I talked about in the first chapter, we read and write in a variety of ways, using a variety of tools, for a variety of purposes. While reading and writing are composed of a range of skills, no one is born a good reader and writer; we work at learning and developing our reading and writing over time. You may be an excellent reader who enjoys long, dense classics but who has trouble understanding scientific materials. You may have a student who is an excellent persuasive writer but who really struggles with writing creatively.

Thinking about the components of literacy as more than these single skills led to a research focus called the New Literacy Studies, headed by Brian Street, Shirley Brice Heath, and others in the 1980s and 1990s. What they found in their work was that literacy can be defined by things like settings, texts, events, and tools—so that literacy, instead of being just reading and writing, can be thought of in terms of multiple "practices." Street (1993), whose research took place in Iran, found that the literacy practices in Muslim religious schools, called *makhtabs*, was very different than that in the U.N.–sponsored schools. The U.N. schools used a more traditional Western reading and writing curriculum where students read and wrote independently. In contrast, students in the Iranian religious schools read aloud chorally, working from a shared text, and oral call-

and-response practices were much more valued than individual reading and written response. Very different practices were valued in very different ways.

Our students engage in a wide variety of literacy practices, even within schools. There are literacy practices associated with science class, like the specialized vocabulary (what James Gee [1996] calls "discourses") and formats of lab reports; oral presentations of artists and artwork in art class; and performances and memorization in drama. At home, students write emails, text on their cell phones, post to their Facebook pages, write and read lists and notes left by their parents, and much more. All of us read an inordinate amount of text each day—from ads and electronic messages to visual texts and signs. Each of these practices uses particular texts and different discourses in certain ways.

By thinking of literacy as literacy practices or literacies, plural instead of singular, we can start to unravel some of the relationships between texts, spaces, tools, and purposes. Students can be more aware of audience, purpose, and voice when they realize that they don't write everything the same way because not everything they write serves the same purpose. The same is true for reading. The nonfiction texts we use one week in a unit on memoir or the Holocaust should be read and understood very differently than the texts in a unit on Shakespeare or poetry. We have different purposes when we teach with different texts; our literacy classes encompass a range of practices.

Using a literacy framework recognizes the various ways literacies come into play in education and the world. Literacy practices are bigger than reading and writing text, although that is central to what they do. Literacies also mean making sense of visual and iconic text (texts that make use of icons), nonverbal and other cues, and more, including the contexts in which we read and write. Thinking of teaching *literacies* recognizes how much we teach when we teach *literacy*, especially in a world where different kinds of texts and forms proliferate. Most important, understanding literacies as multiple practices is essential when it comes to getting at the interaction of new technologies and new literacies.

What Are New Literacies?

New literacies are those new literacy practices that result from a combination of new tools—like instant messaging (IM) and cell phones—and the new kinds of things we can do with them, like texting and chatting (Lankshear and Knobel 2006). It's important to consider both of these aspects because it is possible to take new technologies and do the same kinds of things with them we've always done. Think, for example, of word processing. If you use it just like you would use a typewriter, or perhaps add the spell-check, it doesn't really constitute a new literacy. With a word processer, like a typewriter, you can type a paper, print it out, and turn it in (putting aside for the moment the ability to save the paper, edit it, etc.). Compare that with texting. When we use a cell phone to text a message, we use the affordances of the phone to create an entirely new practice. Yes, we're sending a message, but unlike writing notes or other literacy practices that came before, the capabilities of the cell phone allow us to send the message across long distances, whereas with a note we would have to be in the same geographical space in order to give it to the recipient. As well, a whole new language has emerged around texting, comprised mainly of abbreviations, because the medium of texting must be quick and succinct. Cell phones weren't originally designed for texting; the practice came about because the phone allowed for it, and now people send hundreds of texts each day.

That makes texting an excellent example of a new literacy, in that a new tool—namely, the cell phone, combined with its ability to send short, text-based messages, has allowed us to create a new form of communication that many of us now depend on in communicating with the people in our lives. The literacy practice of texting itself is different from writing a full letter or even an email in that it is immediate and abbreviated, can be playful or informational, crosses any geographical distance instantly, and even supplants voice conversations in some cases (think of the times when it is easier to send a text message than trying to reach someone on the phone). Now we can choose texting from among a variety of communication media when we want to get a message to someone, taking into account the purpose and audience. Too, texting is subversive in that it can and often does take place when your focus is supposed to be on something else—during work, school, in a meeting, and so on.

Another new literacy practice is digital video. Digital video is video that has been digitized, or translated, into a form that allows it to be played through a computer, usually online. When it is played online, it can be shared with an audience, and amateur filmmakers can create digital videos that potentially reach huge numbers. In 2009, YouTube surpassed 100 million viewers in the United

States alone. YouTube is a site that allows anyone who creates an account (which is free and requires only a valid email address) to either upload or view digital video. Not only can users of the site view and/or upload video, they can comment on it through either a typed remark or a video comment.

What makes this a new literacy? First, the ability to create and upload digital videos means that anyone with a video camera, computer, and Internet connection can post videos that can be viewed all over the world; in this sense, home movies and other creations can be published to the world at large. Second, the establishment of a community of users means that the videos aren't simply viewed but are commented on in an ongoing stream of communication that becomes a part of the conversation about the video. You're not just showing your cute video of your baby dancing at a party at your house; you're uploading it to tens of millions of people who can potentially see and comment on it, forwarding the link to their friends and creating a web of critique and connections around it. This kind of creation and connection is unique to the affordances of digital video and a site like YouTube, which allows videos from any user. For the most part, there is no gatekeeper; users can post and enjoy cute animal videos, political ads, educational videos and, yes, inappropriate material. The digital tools of video and a Web-publishing site combine with the practices of creating digital video, posting it, and commenting on it to create a new practice whereby millions tell their stories through visual media. Local bands post homemade music videos, educators post interview clips, families post vacation videos, and teens post their own filmmaking projects, among other things.

In understanding new literacies, it's important to think about how digital tools create the opportunity for new practices through the original applications they can offer. What are the possibilities of these tools? If you choose, for instance, to use blogs with your students, how do they create the kinds of new literacies that will support your students' reading and writing, as compared to other tools and practices you might incorporate?

As teachers, we want to create and incorporate practices that have meaningful content and skills for our students. Texting and YouTube are good examples of new literacies, but you may be wondering what they have to do with your classroom. I use them because their purposes are fairly clear: it's easy to see how texting has led to a practice that is immediate, has shaped a new sort of language use, and makes use of these ubiquitous cell phones. You can also easily see how texting quickly became embedded in the literacies of many of our students and even ourselves.

The same is true of YouTube. Most of us have visited the site and, while our visits may not have been for academic purposes, the power to create and post something of our own seems very clear. My point in using these examples is not to advocate for teaching texting or using YouTube indiscriminately in class but to show how new technologies and their potential for new applications can lead to new literacies very naturally. As humans, we make use of the things we have in order to make meaning in our lives. Literacies are as natural to us as breathing. We want to comprehend our world, and we will use any tools we can in order to do so. In this digital age, we have such a wide variety of tools and media to choose from that it only makes sense to incorporate these new literacies into our teaching too, in order to address the issues of motivation, interest, relevance, cognitive development, community, identity, and safety that we struggle with.

Another aspect of new literacies to keep in mind is the texts that arise from new technologies and new practices. We are bombarded with them every day—text messages, emails, Web pages, ads (in print and on television), books, newspapers, magazines, signs, email messages, and so on. New literacies are expanding the variety of texts we see; just think of the kinds of texts we saw ten years ago, in 2000. Text messaging was not as prevalent, and we didn't carry phones with GPS mapping information in real time. Most of us walked away from our email; we didn't carry it with us. Web pages looked different and we mostly got content from them instead of adding content to them. No one had heard of MySpace or Facebook—two other great examples of new technological tools whose affordances (the ability to create pages that represent the self and connect to others, and the ability to upload information in a variety of formats about yourself, including pictures, video, and sound) have led to new literacies. How are we preparing our students to interact with these texts as they become more and more prevalent? How do we manage to sift through all of them to get the information we need each day?

Thinking about new literacies as a teacher as well as a member of a world shaped by these new technologies and new practices means thinking more deeply about the technologies that are woven through our daily lives before choosing which ones to integrate into your teaching.

It's essential to understand the notion of new literacies because these are the literacies our students know and value, as well as the literacies they will be expected to master once they complete their schooling. While we may not agree with all the practices our students engage in, new literacies are related in the ways they make use of new technologies that are instantaneous, connective, informational, communicative, and reliant on the reading and writing practices of our students.

Reading and writing are more important than ever before, as is the ability to think critically about message, purpose, and audience. Our students may know how to use tools like texting and Facebook, but that doesn't mean they have thought through all the repercussions of their use—the things they post on their Facebook page or the pictures they email. Their practices tend to be limited in terms of the reading and writing they can do. We can introduce them to other practices and tools, such as blogs, wikis, and digital storytelling, that will challenge them to deepen their thinking, reading, and writing.

The following sections outline some of the new literacies of students and their potential connections to the literacy classroom as well as questions they raise for all of us in the fields of literacy and education. I also expand new literacies to include work in visual literacy and information literacy—two increasingly essential concepts in the literacy classroom that are falling to a greater degree under the purview of literacy teachers. In a way, this chapter is a snapshot of some of the things our students are doing and of the potential implications for their literacy practices as well as our teaching. The world, it is a' changin', but we can help shape that change and give our students powerful tools and perspectives on how to be a part of it.

Literacies That Are New in Kind

New literacies, in one sense, are about the new ways we can create and share what we think and do. This section explores current forms of writing such as instant messaging and texting, modern forms of publication such as fan fiction and blogs, and new forms of interacting and being online such as online virtual worlds and communities. All of these represent new and distinct literacies because what they allow us to do is different from what we did before.

Take instant messaging and texting. These are both ways of chatting or communicating with someone else through writing, either synchronously or in real time. The closest version of this that came before IM and text messaging is note passing! But unlike notes, synchronous communication, such as IM and texting, allows us to "talk" instantaneously with someone who is not present with us in the same space. My use of the word *talk* is intentional as well—the communication we do with these media is much more like an oral conversation than a written one. Texts and IM chats often forego conventions like punctuation, capitalization, and conventional spelling. The messages are often sent as staccato phrases instead of complete sentences and both media rely heavily on abbreviations—and these abbreviations have been picked up on and integrated into spoken language, advertising, and even a series of young adult books written entirely in IM language (for example, *ttyl* by Lauren Myracle, a book in a young adult fiction series written entirely as IM conversations). Writing, in these cases, has been shaped by the affordances of these tools, but it bleeds over into other writing. We have all seen abbreviations misused by students in school papers and other assignments. Our students are learning how to use language differently to communicate using different media, but they have yet to think carefully and reflectively about which genres fit which tools and messages.

As well, even though text messages and IMs are carried on with a give-and-take informality like a conversation, they are written texts that can be saved, re-sent, and showed to others. This makes them a record of what went on—something that is captured in a permanent sense, unlike an oral conversation. Our students don't usually consider this fact, and yet many of them are burned by IMs or texts that come back to haunt them after they are posted on MySpace pages or shown to other friends, boyfriends or girlfriends, even parents or teachers. Our students need to understand that these conversations can be more or less permanent, which makes these interactions less like conversations and more like written exchanges, complete with any obscenities, name-calling, or anything else they choose to include. In a way, talking about the potential for a text message or an IM to come back and bite you is an essential lesson on the inherent power of the written word—it's hard to take back or deny something written for anyone to see—and it's also a good lesson for thinking about purpose, message, and audience.

Another new literacy practice takes its form from an older practice, creative writing, but adds the affordances of online publishing and community. This literacy pushes the envelope in terms of writing and feedback. I'm talking about the development of huge online communities devoted to fan fiction, or writing and rewriting popular stories posted to online websites where fans read each other's work and give extensive feedback. Sites devoted to Harry Potter and The Fellowship of the Ring, among others (www.harry potterfanfiction.com or www.fanfiction.net) have huge memberships; members write stories based on the overall plotline of their favorite books, movies, graphic novels, and television shows. These creative works often take a new direction from the established story line—for instance, having Harry fall for Hermione—and are posted to fan sites for others to read. Readers then post feedback for the author, many times giving extensive advice concerning the writing, tone, voice, content, and more. Fans spend hours working on their stories, as researcher Rebecca Black (2005) found, often mirroring the kinds of writing we as teachers would like to see our students do: drafting stories, posting drafts, and revising based on feedback. Student fans also read other stories and learn new techniques for writing as well as how to give useful feedback for a writer. None of this is required reading or writing; members of fan fiction sites, many of whom write multiple stories several pages in length, are doing this work just because they are so fascinated with the fictional worlds represented in their favorite books, movies, and television shows.

Members of fan fiction sites learn an enormous amount about publication and pleasing an audience, because the feedback their stories receive tends to be honest and, in many cases, quite detailed. As well, many fan fiction sites allow users to post illustrations to their stories and give feedback on the drawings, tying together written and visual forms of literacy and teaching students how illustrations work to add to or detract from the overall message of a creative work. Fan fiction writers continually hone their craft and are both intrinsically and extrinsically motivated through the love of the content and comments from others. Many writers on the site go on to write extensively on their own, perhaps writing novels and short stories unrelated to the fan fiction content. From the perspective of teaching literacy, what could be better than a place that allows and encourages students to write and publish their work while also giving them a venue to learn to edit and evaluate writing through useful commentary?

Interestingly, some of the fan fiction that is written concerns characters from video games, an area that would seem to have little or nothing to do with new literacies. Yet James Gee, among others, argues that learning and playing video games does, in fact, have a lot to do with the kinds of new literacies that our students engage in and that are important to learning and communicating today. For many of our students, gaming takes up a significant amount of their time, not just in playing, but in learning and talking about it. As gaming becomes more interactive, students are playing with each other through online networks that stretch across the globe. More important, our students want to learn how to play the game well, which means they spend time not just play-ing it but researching it.

First, players need to learn the vocabulary or discourse of the game—not unlike learning the discourse of science, as I mentioned earlier. They learn this vocabulary by playing it, true, but they also learn it by talking with others and reading about the game (Gee 2007). Many gamers spend hours online reading about their games and learning cheats and tricks. Some become so expert in the game that they learn how to modify, or "mod," the game by reprogram-ming it to do different things. This kind of expertise is largely self-taught; it requires the ability to do online research, to locate important information from among a huge range of websites and online communities, and to ask the right kinds of questions. Gaming is a new literacy in that gamers combine their playing with research skills and literacy practices, often in online communities both by reading and posting, to learn how to play the game better. They also use traditional literacy skills—they read game magazines and inserts and write cheats of their own. Gaming, once thought of as a brain-deadening activity, might actually be a very active kind of learning that involves new and tradi-tional literacies in learning more about the games, modifying them, and partic-ipating in online communities around game playing.

Another new literacy involves the existence and use of virtual, three-dimensional worlds like those in Teen Second Life and Second Life. Online virtual worlds allow a user to create a free account and an avatar—a representation of the user that can go to a three-dimensional space and interact with others. Again, at first glance, this might seem to have little to do with new literacies; however, reading and writing are central to the experience of being on these sites. Online virtual worlds are very new, and their applications for education are still being explored, but one thing is certain: students are drawn to spaces where they can represent themselves and interact with others (just think of the popularity of MySpace and Facebook). Most of this interaction takes place by moving your avatar around, not unlike playing a video game, and typing in a window to chat with others. (There is the option to use a microphone to talk with one another, but typed chat is still the most common method.)

As well, online virtual worlds are embedded with texts, often called notecards, which give information to those navigating the environment. In a space owned by Montclair State University, Professor Laura Nicosia teaches a course on literature that uses space in Second Life to explore the books *The Handmaid's Tale* and *Mama Day*. Students go into the space, which is designed to look like the setting for each of the books, and click on links that provide descriptions from the book. For students who have difficulty visualizing when reading, a three-dimensional environment can create any kind of setting you need, thus providing students with a space to explore what being in the book would have been like. Other spaces in Second Life, which boasts more than eleven million members worldwide, are devoted to Tinturn Abbey and gothic literature, the Sistine Chapel, the Library of Congress, and many more.

Through new kinds of practices like these, unique literacies develop. We can write in a way that is almost like talking, yet is also writing. We can become a member of a fan community and rewrite our favorite stories, then get feedback on what we have written. We can learn about game playing and become better players, as well as learn programming, modifications, and how to gain a new technology. We can even explore the settings and spaces of novels and places from all over the world—all by using reading and writing in innovative ways. While you may not make use of any of these practices in your teaching, they are excellent examples of the new kinds of "stuff" we can do with new literacies, and where we might be heading in the future.

From Web 1.0 to 2.0

One way to understand the new tools available to us and our students is to understand the shifts the Web has gone through since its inception, or at least since most of us began using it in the early to mid 1990s. At that point, most of the time we used the Internet (I use the terms the *Internet* and the *World Wide Web* interchangeably, although some might argue that the Web is a subset of the Internet) either to send electronic mail or to get information. Leaving email aside, although it certainly was an innovation that has changed the way we communicate, we connected to the Web through our phone modems (remember that sound of the dial-up modem?) in order to log on through Netscape, the most common browser before Internet Explorer. When we got to Netscape, mostly what we did was look up information. Here, as never before, most of us had access to more information more quickly and from wherever we happened to be connecting. We no longer had to go in to a library to use their electronic databases, which were usually on CD-ROMs; instead we could connect from the office or even from home to a huge array of information resources.

Bill Gates, the founder of Microsoft, called this ability of the Internet "IAYF," or Information at Your Fingertips, and he and his company worked to capitalize on the expertise of the Internet to create more and better ways to get the information to us. This, then, was Web 1.0—the ability of the Internet to get us more information than ever before, and the manner in which we searched out, sifted through, and made use of the information we received.

While the Internet's information capabilities are still central to what we do online, we have moved into a new iteration of the Web, called Web 2.0. Think of the first version of the Web, Web 1.0, as manifest in Netscape, Internet Explorer, and sites like Ofoto, which sold services for transferring your photos from a digital format onto paper. Now think of free services like Flickr, where users can create a free account and put up photos to share with anyone, anywhere. Or YouTube, which allows for free video sharing. Now, for searching, we have Google, which is free—and has a wide variety of search engines for academic articles (Google Scholar), blogs (Google Blogs), and shopping, among others. There's a free browser (Firefox) so you no longer have to purchase Explorer as a part of Microsoft software.

Web 2.0 is marked by technologies and tools that are free and allow the user to create content, share it with others, and make it publicly available. No longer are we restricted to buying services or just finding information. It used to be that in order to publish online, users had to know how to create and code a website, have a server on which to host it, and so on. Now we have free services like Blogger that take all the hard work out of it. As I will show you in Chapter 4, creating and posting a blog is as easy as using a word processing software. Blogger and other free online sites do all the coding and hosting.

This shift is important, not just in terms of how we see the Web as a place that is more than a site to gather information, but in how we can use it within and beyond the classroom. The Internet is now the largest and easiest place not only to gather information but also to publish material, comment on work, communicate, and participate in learning and other communities. Doing these things definitely constitutes new literacies because these practices take new tools, like blogs, and create original practices. Consider digital storytelling, for example. Our students can learn about digital stories by visiting the Center for Digital Storytelling (www.storycenter.org). They can write and film their own stories, and then publish them. They can comment on each other's stories, and learn peer communication and critique. All of these are Web 2.0 practices that invite our students and ourselves to be creators, innovators, and critics— important stances that help our students take active roles in their literacies and build on their expertise with digital technologies.

Many Web 2.0 technologies are also multimodal, meaning they make use of multiple modes—visual, aural, written, and iconic—in a single text. Digital stories may have video, still images, music, oral commentary, and icons. Blogs may include pictures, links, or embedded video. In contrast to most of the texts created for traditional classroom assessments, new literacies not only allow for multiple modes but, in fact, encourage them. Nearly every Web page we and our students come into contact with has multiple modes. Look, for example, at the front page of the online *New York Times*. It includes the first paragraph (or graph) of the top stories, along with headlines that are links to the entire story, photos that are also links, interactive ads, slideshows, video, links to blogs from *New York Times* bloggers, lists of the top blogged and emailed stories, and links to podcasts. Unlike reading the front page of the traditional paper *New York Times*, which is a static text, the electronic version is hypertextual and multimodal. More and more of the texts we read, and will be expected to produce, have this capability, so it's important to understand the affordances of electronic tools and to make space for them in our teaching and in our students' work.

Multimodal texts can be overwhelming (certainly the online *New York Times* is a good example of that), but properly applied, the use of multiple modes can support varied learning styles. Embedded links in a page or blog can take a reader to more information that can support or extend learning; a video can help a reader visualize the text or get to know the author or the setting. Teaching our students how to make use of multiple modes in their writing could help them refer directly to the sources of their information or ideas. Because our students are comfortable with multimodal texts—as seen in the amount of reading they do online and the popularity of graphic novels, magazines, and comic books as reading materials—forms of texts that support the written material with visual information and icons can be particularly helpful for readers who struggle with comprehension (Frey and Fisher 2008).

We know from our teaching experience that applying multiple modes can help keep our students from being distracted—from a simple overhead, which displays a larger, visual representation of written material, to using films and video, pictures, audio, and other resources. Multimodal tools build on the same idea but pack more than one mode into the same instrument. Our students, being the multitaskers they are, have little trouble with this, but we can help them to slow down and use these different modes in other ways such as podcasting.

A podcast is a simple audio broadcast that has been digitized and uploaded to the Internet, allowing other people to listen. Many educational podcasts, available through iTunes for free if you want to check them out, are created by teachers using a free software called Audible. A podcast, or a video podcast (which is the same thing but using video instead of audio), focuses usually on a single topic, so students have to slow down and listen or watch. Because of the multimodal applications of Web 2.0, you can embed links to podcasts of your own or produced by someone else in a class blog or wiki. Podcasts can capture a lecture, a minilesson, a student presentation or book review, and much more. They build on students' abilities to learn information orally and make that information available to students anywhere an Internet connection exists, not just in the classroom, so podcasts can be a great way to reinforce information for students.

All these kinds of resources may take time for you to get used to, both for yourself and in your teaching. That's all right—it takes a while to become comfortable with the affordances of each and, once done, to sift the wheat from the chaff in terms of your classroom's needs. In the appendix to this book, you will find a list of good websites to check out, which can help you think about and try new kinds of multimodal resources that are useful for teaching, and learning about teaching, both literacy and technology. In teaching new literacies, it's essential to become familiar with them yourself.

Communities Online: Where Many of Us Fear to Tread

One place where many of us fear to go, perhaps because of the hype surrounding them, is online communities. The two most famous (or infamous) are MySpace and Facebook. Both boast more than 100 million members; early in 2009, Facebook released information that it had reached more than 150 million members, making its community larger than many small countries, and stating that its reach had become global.

Now let me be very clear. I am not advocating that we should be making use of MySpace or Facebook in the classroom per se. But membership and use are an important part of the new literacies that our students engage in every day. Yep, our students are on them, whether we think it's a good idea or not. To that end, it makes sense to understand what these communities are and how they work.

MySpace and Facebook are both social networking sites, built so that people could get to know one another online. A person signs up for the site for free and creates a personal page that represents him or her and includes a wide variety of information. This information can be of concern, since many of our students list personal information—not just their relationship status, but full names, locations, cell phone numbers, and so forth. These pages are also multimodal: on MySpace, students can and do make changes to the page layout, include songs, and have a wide leeway in terms of the visual and aural aspects of their page. Facebook, by contrast, holds users to a form of personal page so that all pages look alike, but both sites allow users to post a wide range of information, pictures, status updates (what you are doing right now), and more.

One of the most essential things to understand about social networking sites is that students accrue huge friend lists. It is not uncommon for students to add as friends anyone who asks, so students' pages may boast friend lists that number in the several hundreds. This means that everyone on that list gets an update when the student changes his or her page, particularly on Facebook, which is quickly becoming the social network of choice for teens. Originally, social networking sites like the long-dormant Friendster were designed for people in their twenties and included warnings about adding personal information. Facebook came out of Harvard and was created by a group of friends who wanted to put their university facebook, or list of new students, online. The idea caught on like wildfire.

But Facebook is not just a community of teenagers. It is used by teens and adults for a wide variety of reasons. At my university, everyone from first-year students to associate deans is on it (making for an interesting reflection before you post anything, at least from my standpoint as a faculty member). Many of us use Facebook to keep in touch with and even work with colleagues in the field from all over the country and the world. Facebook allows users to create groups that range from the silly ("I Love Jon Stewart") to the more serious ("Barack Obama for President") and, indeed, there is some preliminary evidence that Facebook played a role in the last presidential election in increasing the voting rate among voters under the age of twenty-five.

Whether or not you choose to be a member of a social networking community, understanding how they work is essential. Your students create a page to represent themselves and add friends. Over time, they also add photos, interests, quotes, links, and more. These pages allow for conversations between friends, status updates, and links between people. Your students often "friend" people they know in person as well as people they have never met. The thing to keep in mind for anyone on a social networking site is that, like an IM, email, or anything written using a computer—it never completely goes away.

Our students use writing online already to represent themselves, so writing to a blog or a wiki is a natural connection to make for them, once we point out how language is used in both. A blog isn't a personal website in the same way that a profile on MySpace or Facebook is, but what is written there does represent the writer, thereby building on their technological expertise.

New literacies may seem transitory, but they are an indelible part of our students' lives. As they create, communicate, and post more online, we will need to understand how new literacies stretch across their lives, make use of multiple modalities, and have both positive and negative consequences. This can help us make decisions about what we want to use in our classrooms and how we will do it.

Other Essential Literacies

One of the literacies that overlap with new literacies but has its roots in the past is visual literacy. Arguably, visual literacy—the practice of making sense of visual information—has been around since the days of hieroglyphics and illuminated manuscripts. Much of the meaning we make and take from the world is done in the form of pictures, both with and without written language. This has always been true, but perhaps never more so than now, when so many new forms of media exist that can create and use visual images. Frey and Fisher (2008), in *Teaching Visual Literacy: Using Comic Books, Graphic Novels, Anime, Cartoons, and More to Develop Comprehension and Thinking Skills*, argue that today we live in an increasingly visual world but fail to take that fact into account in our classes. Our students are immersed in images that can be "read" in a variety of ways and that directly impact the sense we make of the written texts that accompany them. All of this contributes to comprehension, according to Frey and Fisher: "We think of visual literacy as describing the complex act of meaning making using still or moving images. As with reading comprehension, visually literate learners are able to make connections, determine importance, synthesize information, evaluate, and critique" (1). This means that meaning making incorporates multiple sign systems, as discussed earlier in thinking about multimodality, and that visual literacy is an important component of literacy practices, especially digital literacies, where visual elements are key.

Think of nearly anything you read or interact with online. Not only does it probably have a picture or two, it might include an embedded video—a practice that is becoming increasingly popular as more and more people learn how to create and upload videos. More than that, online pages aren't laid out as primarily textual, like in a book. Color, links, layout, and other elements are changeable, and there exists no standard to which all pages must adhere. Consequently, nearly every page we encounter can and often does look different, so we must learn to interact with it differently and figure out how to make sense of its visual and written information (as well as any icons embedded in the pages and the browser). These different sign systems—visual, written, and iconic—signal different information, and some students may need help making decisions about what information to attend to, how to create online texts that work, and how to use all the different tools and systems at their disposal.

Interestingly, the prevalence of visual information can help struggling readers form mental images and understand texts that otherwise might be too difficult. Embedded photos and video can offer additional information that helps develop an understanding of the material, especially for those students who have the most difficulty in comprehending primarily written texts. Online sources of information, with their multiple modes, may serve those students best who need additional support by providing extensions and visual information. In addition, images are engaging and motivating, and online, interactive, visual texts are more likely to draw some students in than traditional, static, primarily verbal texts. While many of us, as teachers, are not only more familiar but very comfortable with losing ourselves in the printed word, many of our students are attracted to the interactivity, visuals, and even the movement of online texts. Knowing this can help explain why using online resources to support traditional texts in the classroom is not an additional task but an important way to engage our students who struggle with reading, motivation, and engagement.

The visual aspects of online texts and new literacies are a crucial support when it comes to dealing with the amount of information available online, too. One of the issues with integrating new literacies into the classroom, as well as in understanding new literacies in our everyday lives, is the sheer volume of information available to us at any given time. Our email inboxes are filled to overflowing; a Google search turns up hundreds of thousands of hits. Everything we read or see on TV has a website counterpart to it, with the URL prominently displayed. Our friends and family send photos and links daily, sometimes hourly. If you're on a social network, you're getting constant updates as to what your friends are doing. If you Twitter (a new micro-blogging tool explained in greater detail in Chapter 6), you're getting instant updates from the people whom you follow (and who are telling you what they had for breakfast or what they watched on TV last night). Your phone is filled with voice mails and text messages and you can't find or even remember receiving that important email you need to respond to, no later than yesterday.

We're living not only in an information overload society, but in what Lankshear and Knobel (2006) have termed an "attention economy." Somehow we have to determine what we can pay attention to and when, because it just isn't possible to take it all in. And we have to impart this skill to our students—because they need to learn how to choose from among the many targets of their attention to find the information they need. One way to do this quickly is to use the visual information—photos, scanning a site, and such—to determine whether the site contains the information you need. Another is to begin to warehouse or collect valuable resources on blogs and wikis so that your students don't have to continually go out to the larger Web to look for information. You can keep what you have found most valuable for your students to use in a central location. And you can teach students to synthesize the information they have acquired into a post that is useful for them and their peers, such as on a blog or within a digital story.

So What Does All This Have to Do with Blogs, Wikis, and Digital Stories?

Blogs, wikis, and digital stories are three examples of new literacies that make use of visual literacy. They combat information overload by acting as filter systems, pushing students to choose and synthesize what is most important for the task at hand. They use new tools—blogs, wikis, and the ability to shoot video and edit digitally and post or publish the result online—to engage students in new practices: writing and publishing to the World Wide Web in an authentic way. Students can create written and visual texts using all three tools, building on their literacy abilities to extend their new literacies within and beyond the classroom. In a world that has shifted from Web 1.0 to Web 2.0, blogs, wikis, and digital stories are three ways you can integrate new literacies into your teaching at various levels that work for you, and then progressively increase use of these resources as you become more familiar with them.

In any class, we start with what we know. As literacy teachers, we work with our students on reading and writing mostly traditional written texts—readers, essays, accepted literature. So how do we move from more traditional practices to integrating new literacies in the classroom? The best first step may be for students to take their writing within the classroom to the next level: publishing it online, in a blog or a wiki.

Our students, of course, do not create texts in a vacuum. In traditional literacies used in class assignments, students have always written for an audience. Yet that audience was, and still is, limited at best. Most of the time, students write for their teacher and for their grade, an extrinsic motivator that rates them in relation to each other or becomes a personal competition or reminder of failure. Some teachers using a writing workshop approach have students "publish" pieces by reading them aloud, creating a classroom publication, or posting them, which does move publication closer to an authentic experience by providing the possibility of a wider audience.

As compared to authors who write for a living, and publish to a larger, often unknown audience, publication in a classroom is a limited experience that only reaches peers in that setting or the school. True publication means putting your work out where people beyond your immediate sphere can read it. New technologies allow our students to experience authentic publication, through websites devoted to student writing, student and classroom blogs, digital story sites, and more. Students' words can have a much bigger impact, even if only implied, when they are put out through technology to the world at large.

Our students know this, since the potential to reach many people is one of the main draws to participating in social networking sites, blogging, creating videos, and posting photos with stories. Being able to write something that will reach a wider audience is intrinsically attractive. Students can show friends and family and, of course, there is the potential to reach a much wider audience than that. As discussed in the first chapter to this book, our students are presented with many extrinsic motivators that may or may not work on them: grades, family pressures, class standing, college acceptance, staying in advanced or gifted courses, being able to play sports, and so on. Yet anything that is intrinsically motivating to a student is more likely to be lasting and authentic. Knowing that something you wrote is good enough for people to read and talk about is exciting.

Another way that traditional literacy practices can create a bridge to new literacy practices is through the motivating aspect of using technology itself. Most "real" writers use some form of technology, whether it be a word processing program, a website that solicits response from readers, a blog or wiki, or an online publication venue (the *New York Times* publishes a much more complete newspaper, including several blogs from guest bloggers and *Times* staffers online than it does with its paper version). When we ask our students to write something out in longhand, then rewrite it for every revision, we take away the tools we have at our disposal. Regardless of whether you believe in the use of spell-check or not, writing on a computer is, for most people, faster and easier. You can edit much more easily on a screen because you can pick up and move chunks of text or delete without having to rewrite the entire piece. Our students are surrounded by publications that are done through word processing even if they are not professionally published, and they often draw a distinction between "real" writing and school writing. For them, real writing uses professional tools.

Another distinction our students often see between "real" writing and school-based writing tasks is that the topics of school papers are usually forced on the writer. The traditional writer's workshop model allows students to choose their own topics, but in this day and age of standardized testing, many of us have begun assigning topics that will aid our students in meeting certain standards and benchmarks. This makes perfect sense, but if the only writing students are doing is on assigned subject matter, the interest they have in writing itself sharply decreases. In informal writing venues, students have more freedom to choose. If you've always had your students write journals, for example, why not have them write personal blogs? You can decide whether these will be restricted solely to communication between class members, but students may very well embrace writing more if they get to do it using a computer, with a theme or idea of their choice. As well, you could assign students in pairs to read each other's posts and comment on them. This is much more public than a journal, and gives students a reason for sustained, regular writing practice. You can determine whether spelling or grammar count, and students can use the venue of a blog to try out new ideas and write through a variety of issues and subjects.

Overall, integrating technology into writing instruction and practice just makes sense. It motivates our students, allows them to create the types of texts (multimodal, hypertextual) that they will be expected to create later, and gives them a much larger audience than they would have with a school assignment alone. Integrating technology moves instruction closer to the authentic means of communication and creation that are favored in the digital world. In particular, blogs, wikis, and digital stories are free or low-cost tools that integrate technology in practical ways in a writing program or language arts curriculum.

The same holds true for reading. Much of the reading we have students do for our classes comes from assigned texts, usually class novels drawn from what is known as the canon of accepted literature, or other materials we cobble together to support the existing materials we have. If we limit ourselves to the printed materials contained in the classroom, there is no way we can meet the reading levels and interests of all the students in our classrooms at the moment. But if we start to incorporate materials that we find online—all kinds of texts from short stories and poems to visual texts and nonfiction articles—we can begin to satisfy the interests and levels of all of the students in front of us. Moreover, we can introduce our students to a wider world than we could otherwise have done, and we can bring in video and audio resources from all over the world to deepen our students' understanding of the topics we teach, like writing persuasively, the Holocaust, ancient history, memoir, and much more.

Jason Ohler (2007), the author of *Digital Storytelling in the Classroom: New Media Pathways to Literacy, Learning, and Creativity*, makes a compelling case that all new media take the form of stories to better teach our students. We can introduce them to the tenets of media literacy, like reading more critically and being more aware of the media we consume online, as well as how to create a persuasive online message.

Ohler also makes the point that new media contain components of traditional forms of writing and that, in order to create stories using new media, our students must be familiar with traditional aspects of literature like setting, characters, problem, climax, resolution, and so on. Being literate today means being able to map an understanding of the components of texts across a variety of media—both online and off—through being familiar with what these media have in common and what they do not. Ohler writes, "Having students blend reading the classics in print with experiencing more contemporary works in new media form ideally situates them to be literate in the most useful, contemporary sense" (2007, 47).

Moreover, having students learn to create in new media allows them to begin to understand how new media can be constructed to persuade, Ohler points out. New media span a vast range of genres; for our students to be truly media literate, they need to be critically aware of the ways these genres shape messages in order to parse these messages and understand the underlying forces at play: "In an age in which media companies see young people largely in terms of market share, having the ability to read print and nonprint text critically is a matter of survival" (47).

Our students live in a world marked by a shift into new literacies yet we, as teachers, have been trained to teach and learn through traditional literacy practices. The world is changing around us, and we are changing what we do as a part of it. It makes sense that our teaching transform as well and we shift from the traditional ways we teach and learn to begin to incorporate new literacies into our classrooms. The next chapter will present examples of wikis, blogs, and digital stories being used by teachers and classes around the world to support literacy teaching and learning in this new, brave world.

What Are Blogs, Wikis, and Digital Stories?

3

When using technological tools with your students, particularly Web 2.0 tools, certain things work better than others. First and foremost, any teacher must have a reason for using technology in his or her teaching. It's not enough that the school just bought SmartBoards or that your principal has heard about wikis. In order to integrate technologies effectively, you must choose the tool that fits the use, as we talked about at the end of Chapter 2, and have a philosophy for technology integration. If you want an online repository of information from and for the class, then creating a course wiki makes perfect sense. From a front page, you can create and link to pages of resources, student papers, and uploaded files, including lectures, while carrying on an ongoing conversation. If you want an avenue for students to write and publish their thinking, create a writing community around particular ideas, learn to comment and critique each other's work, and reflect on their growth over time, a blog may be a perfect choice. And if you want a group of students to create a collaborative, multimedia narrative that moves from a written to a multimodal text, a digital story will fit the bill best of all. Any of the tools listed in this book will work at different parts of the reading and writing process and in the literacy classroom. It's just a question of what to choose and how to implement it, as well as knowing how the tool serves your teaching philosophy and needs at that point.

This chapter will define blogs, wikis, and digital stories; the next chapter gives examples of online instances where teachers and students from around the world are using them in real situations. The settings for using blogs, wikis, and digital stories can range from within to across and beyond the classroom to connect groups of students worldwide. Some classrooms using these tools have more technology available to them than others—the thing to remember is that blogs, wikis, and even digital stories can be incorporated into classrooms with only one computer or many. You don't have to have laptops for every child or extensive digital video equipment to create and use these tools with your students; many blogs, wikis, and digital stories can be done with a minimum of technology. Hopefully these examples will give you some ideas of how you might use them yourself, or with your students, for a variety of purposes.

So What Are Blogs, Wikis, and Digital Stories Exactly? How Do They Work?

Blogs, wikis, and digital stories share one thing in common—they are all types of texts (not just written but visual and aural, too) that can be created using free and open tools available online and with most Mac and/or PC computers.

Most of our students are already familiar with these tools to a certain degree—MySpace and Facebook have blog components, many students use Wikipedia to learn about something, and thousands of teens contribute video stories to YouTube and original pieces to fan fiction sites. We need to understand how these forms of writing are important not only in our students' lives but in the evolving information economy in which we live. By using blogs, wikis, and digital stories, we are bridging what students are already doing in their online lives outside of school to how they can use the same digital tools for academic purposes.

First, let's examine how each of these tools functions, look at some good examples of blogs, wikis, and digital stories, and determine the key differences between them.

Blogs

Blogs, shortened from *weblogs*, initially developed as personally authored, open, and free journals or websites available to users (Blood 2002). A blog is simply a website that is authored by a single person or a group and that allows the author or authors to post or publish writing in reverse order so that the most recent posts are first. This is an inversion from the traditional format of diaries or compilations, which puts the oldest information and entries first and then builds up over time. Instead, the focus is put on the most recent, up-to-date information, but a backstory of growth over time is still available—blogs archive older posts so that authors and readers can revisit what was written before, an important factor for teachers and students.

Another key difference between blogs and traditional compilations is that readers can not only read blogs by anyone who has access to them (access can range from being completely open to anyone who can find the blog to being restricted to an invited audience) but also comment on the posts from the author(s). This makes a blog a kind of collaborative text in which authors and readers interact in tangible ways and leave a history of the interaction. Blogs, then, are coauthored by the main author of the blog and the readers who leave comments, and these interactions can become a key part of the blog's content. By using these interactions, teachers can show students how to make appropriate peer comments and offer constructive suggestions; the written format means that the teacher or reader can keep track of these comments and understand them in the context of the blog as a whole.

Blogs began several years ago, but at first were the purview of those who knew how to program a website, according to Rebecca Blood (2002), the author of *The Weblog Handbook* and one of the first bloggers. Her blog, rebecca's pocket, began in 1999 (www.rebeccablood.net) and, like many blogs in the early days of blogging, is more a series of Web links with running commentary offering new and interesting information from a variety of websites covering all sorts of topics. This type of linking blog, however, has generally given way to blogs that are personal accounts of experiences and ideas from all over the world and in every language rather than lists of links; bloggers today write more of the content themselves rather than posting lists of annotated links. Blogs are truly universal; they can and are written by everyone, from young children to the elderly, and ultimately serve as a democratic writing resource available to the world.

Now, even though everyone has the potential to create a free blog using sites like Blogger and Edublogs (Chapter 4 has more on setting up your own blog), and literally millions of blogs have been created, blogs can also be very powerful. Some attract a readership of thousands; for example, during the Iraq war many people became war correspondents of a sort because they used free, open blogs to post eyewitness accounts of the war. These blogs have had an impact on mainstream media as well as on legislative and governmental decision making. The *New York Times* now features staff blogs in the online version of the paper, and political blogs like the *Huffington Post* and the *Drudge Report* have become known for covering both ends of the political spectrum, often breaking news before the mainstream media can.

For example, the scandal surrounding a story reported on by Dan Rather about the military record of then President George W. Bush was broken by political blogs that called into question the accuracy of documents Rather used as his primary sources, according to Wikipedia articles on the Killian memos and a *New York Times* article (Rutenberg 2004). And in 2005, *blog* was named the Word of the Year by Merriam-Webster and added to their dictionary. Blogs run the gamut from little-known websites to powerful sources of information.

Because blogs can incorporate multimedia resources like podcasts, video, and links to other websites, texts that students create can be multimodal, making use of a variety of resources (linking directly to sources can also cut down on plagiarism, since the original source can be so easily reached). In deciding what sources, modes, and links to incorporate, our students can learn to discern what should or should not be incorporated into the texts they create—a skill that is incredibly important in a world becoming rapidly overwhelmed with information. Information is the name of the game, and whether through a blog or another digital text type, our students must know how to locate and use important information.

Blogs began with individuals who wanted to tell their stories or make available important information, like Rebecca Blood or Barbara Ganley, a professor at Middlebury College and one of the best-known educational bloggers working in higher education as well as an accomplished writer and photographer (http://bgblogging.net). Bloggers write about everything from parenting to politics, but education has quickly become a key topic. Today, many teachers blog about their teaching, and their blogs are excellent resources for new teachers or teachers who want to think more about their practice, especially in terms of learning to integrate technology into their teaching.

For example, in the blog A Plethora of Technology, the anonymous author is "dedicated to giving educators a place to gain thought provoking ideas, Web links, teaching suggestions, and a place for the author to vet out ideas" (http://plethoratech.blogspot.com). This Google Certified Teacher posts his or her thoughts about teaching with technology and using multiple intelligences in the classroom, explains how to use the latest technologies such as Twitter's micro-blogging service (more about Twitter can be found in Chapter 6), and offers links to information and videos teachers can use in the classroom. This blog is an example of what might be called a resource and reflection blog: the author is providing resources and links along with reflection targeted at a specific audience; in this case, teachers who are interested in learning to integrate technology into their teaching.

Similarly, the blog Science teacher: Breaking out of the classroom into the world, by a blogger calling himself Doyle, focuses on the process of teaching science and reflecting on the system of education. His description of his blog states, "I love to teach. Science is *not* about content—the content is ephemeral, it's the process that matters" (http://doyle-scienceteach.blogspot.com). Doyle chronicles his adventures in learning to teach using new tools, as well as his own forays into new technologies including Twitter, Facebook, and Google Documents. Much of his blog is a philosophical reflection on the nature of teaching and the role of science in understanding the world, and his blog vacillates between being a chronicle of his experiences and a series of essays on the importance of teaching science in a changing world. But because he chooses to write a blog rather than keep a journal or more private communication, his thoughts are published to the world and readers can and do leave comments—including his colleagues, some of whom are wrestling with the same questions—making this an interesting and valuable source of information and reflection for teachers pondering the same issues.

There are many teachers who are working in the world of educational technology, who find the time to also write blogs on how and why using technology has stepped up their teaching and their students' learning. Will Richardson (http://weblogg-ed.com/), who is well known for his work in the field of educational technology, has compiled an educational blogs list on his website that includes a huge number of teacher blogs that serve as excellent resources for new ideas on how to find new technologies, or integrate the technologies you might already have, for all grades and nearly all subject matters—including literacy. You can find this list at: http://supportblogging.com/Links+to+School+Bloggers#toc6. These teacher blogs cover all levels and subjects, discuss the nuts and bolts of teaching and technology, reflect on their authors' lives as teachers, and include blogs by librarians, technology coordinators, and others. There is much that is inspiring in reading blogs like Diane Cordell's Journey (http://dmcordell.blogspot.com), which includes beautiful photography along with poetry, examples of assignments and activities she has done with her students, poetry for April's National Poetry Month, and connections she has made both online and in person with other amazing teachers.

Blogs are also an excellent way to keep up with high-profile educators who shape the field. Kathy Schrock is well known for her work in the areas of literacy and technology integration in public schools. Her blog, Kathy Schrock's Kaffeeklatsch (http://kathyschrock.net/blog), will keep you updated on new ideas for using technology in your classroom. Well written and presented, Schrock's blog reports on the ideas that she tries on with teachers all over the country, posting her expertise where anyone can benefit from it easily. Other teachers comment on the posts as they try her ideas or raise questions, making this site a veritable cornucopia of information, written in an informal and accessible style.

Teacher blogs are a great way to become a part of a larger community and understand teaching from a variety of perspectives as well as gather resources you can use for your own teaching and learning. For new teachers especially, reading the thoughts of a younger teacher or novice contemporary can be a lifeline, a tangible way to know you're not alone. But blogs aren't limited to teacher-led projects. A blog can also represent a class as a whole, serve as a space to update and keep track of important projects and upcoming assignments, and connect to parents and the community.

Bookwrap, Alisha Cunningham's year 3 classroom blog in Sydney, Australia (http://bookwrap.edublogs.org), uses a class blog to learn more about authors they are reading and includes a space to publish pieces of writing on a companion blog, Wizard Writer's (http://storiesonline.edublogs.org). On the Bookwrap blog, students post comments about the authors and books, including why they liked certain books or a particular author, thereby learning how to talk about reading as part of a reading community. On the other end of the age spectrum, Gary Coyle's grade 8 Humanities class at the American Embassy School in New Delhi, India, uses a class blog with linked student blogs (http://mrcoyle.edublogs.org). The main class blog reviews what was covered each week and posts a question for the students to work on; the students' blogs, which are listed in a sidebar, respond to assigned posts. On the main course blog, other sidebars also list tools that students can use, including a wiki for the humanities course, the CIA World Factbook, Dictionary.com, and many other online resources. Both of these classroom blogs serve as clearinghouses for the classroom where students (and parents) can get information for class projects, publish student writing on a companion blog or individual student blogs, and link to other sites.

Perhaps the most powerful use of a blog is in developing a student's own voice as a writer and thinker. Because blogs are best known as vehicles for a writer to publish his or her thoughts to the world, they allow students to safely learn to think through writing in a way that is public yet part of a learning community—individual yet shared, solo yet interactive. A teacher can take a class blog to the next level by teaching his or her students how to create their own blogs, thereby giving them a voice, a place to write that is their own and that can be individualized and added to, a record of their change over time, and a place to reflect on reading and use writing to think. If you make blogging a part of the school routine, you can build on the natural motivation of adolescents to write in order to make sense of their world while helping them develop the practices of reading and writing more deeply and critically.

Any group of students can use a blog to respond to a question or an idea raised by readings—Susan Callaghan at West Caldwell High School in New Jersey had her students respond to the question: What are your thoughts on arranged marriage? This was in relation to a class reading and film activity in which arranged marriages played a central role. By asking her students to think about and respond to this question, she introduced one of the main topics to be discussed prior to the reading and film. This type of prereading activity notifies students as to what to pay attention to when reading, and primes any prior knowledge they may have.

Other teachers have used blogs as ongoing reviews for students to critique books and readings. Students post in a format that examines and discusses specific writings in order to help them all choose books they will be interested in. Blogs in response to readings can answer questions that arise from those readings, connect ideas from the book to everyday experiences, and link to additional resources and information. I have used course blogs to have students summarize and analyze nonfiction readings as well as review fictional ones, and comment on each other's reviews as well as post their own. Writing a classroom blog is a collaborative experience in the best sense of the word because the blog's meaning changes through the interactions that arise with each post, comment, and link that is published.

Individual blogs take this collaborative experience and give ownership to each specific student. Students design their own blogs—including choosing titles, layout and design, color, and more—and they use these blogs for a variety of purposes. In teaching *The Kite Runner* to incoming freshmen who needed additional reading and writing support, I had students respond to daily questions and issues raised by the readings. These students, including some of the students profiled in the first chapter of this book, disliked reading and writing, particularly for school. Some stated outright that they had never finished a book before. In assigning *The Kite Runner,* I wanted them to be immersed in a book that not only grabbed them but related back to their own experiences. The problem was how to connect the experiences of a boy fleeing war-torn Afghanistan for the United States with those of students from northern New Jersey. It turned out that many of the students in the summer program were recent immigrants, some of whom had to leave their native countries in similar circumstances. Too, the book raises important questions and contains themes of friendship, love, family, and survival that most students could relate to. In their blogs, they wrote their reactions to the main character's behavior toward his best friend, to his relationship with his father, and to their own families and how they compared to those in the story. Students wrote about what they thought were the right actions for the hero to take, and what they felt was wrong. Their posts and feelings were strong and powerful, and the students connected to the book on a deeper level than even I had anticipated.

My reason for using individual blogs instead of a class blog lies in the ownership and authorship that personal blogs gave the students over time. As students added posts, both about the book and other topics that came up in class, their learning and thinking were progressively chronicled. They could look back at all they had done and see how much they had changed from the beginning of the workshop. With older students, even those who are disengaged from reading and writing, a sense of self is central to their literacy. Allowing them a space that is their own to write and design is important in motivating and challenging them—even if you assign the topics of the posts. In this workshop, I began by assigning most of the topics and then moved to allowing more and more "free" topics where students could write about what they liked (as long as it was appropriate for classmates and me to read and comment on).

Part of an individual blog, too, is getting students into a regular writing practice. In this sense, blogging can be like journaling, except that it has a larger audience—and this audience is key in that it challenges students to write something worth reading and commenting on. Commenting on students' personal blogs is also important; students and teachers should comment on these blogs in order to validate what has been written as important and worthwhile. A blog has an implied audience because it is published to the Web, but the audience is really only measured by the comments made and the number of visits a site records, so commenting is just as important to individual blogs as it is to classroom blogs.

Teens have been blogging much longer than many of us realize. Many of the first bloggers were teens using sites like LiveJournal and MySpace (which has a blogging component) to keep their friends up-to-date on their daily lives. As large-scale, free sites like Blogger gained prominence, many teens set up their own blogs and shared the addresses with friends. While the content on these blogs is probably not what you would sanction as a literacy teacher, the idea of writing daily for a specific audience as a literacy practice falls precisely into the kind of practice we do want our students to engage in regularly.

By using blogs along with class websites, we can use the same kinds of practices as a part of our classroom new literacies to get students engaged while also challenging them to think and read more critically.

One excellent example of a student blog, Report from Planet Stas (http://planetstas.blogspot.com), is written by a student who not only uses his blog to keep friends and family updated on his life but as a place to publish his award-winning poetry and photography. As with any blog, he can customize the layout, choose colors and fonts, include photos and links to other information online, embed video, and much more. Unlike a journal or paper publication, using the affordances of a blog means he can share his work with a much wider audience—his poetry and photography can be seen literally around the world—and readers can comment on that work, giving feedback and praise. Stas also posts reviews of shows he has seen (including his first opera) and news about his award nomination as a musician. This is definitely a child who can do it all—and his blog allows him to share it with the world.

Other blog sites, such as TeenInk (www.teenink.com), create spaces for teens to create and post their own blogs, but without the connection to the classroom. While Stas has the initiative to create and maintain a blog on his own, many students might not do so without some sort of outside structure and scaffolding, like that of a literacy classroom. The positive benefits of regularly writing, reading others' work, and learning to comment and critique positively the thoughts others have posted are important skills that are part of literacy learning. If having students create blogs through Blogger or Edublogs is too daunting, using a site like TeenInk might be a better choice. Be aware, however, that the site chooses bloggers, and students have to apply, whereas creating blogs through Blogger and linking them to a class blog gives you as the teacher more control.

There are some concerns with allowing students to blog on their own, certainly. As I discuss in the following chapter, there are blog sites that allow the teacher to link all student blogs to a central class blog and thereby oversee posts before they are made public. As well, when students realize that these blogs are public and part of who they are as writers, they become responsible for the content. Writing a blog is an authentic publishing experience in that the content can be shared with parents, administrators, other teachers, and peers. Students can see that when their words can be easily accessed from any computer with an Internet connection, their persuasive entries might have a larger impact on the world than essays written in a class.

Students in my precollege summer reading program found blogging to be a powerful way to respond thoughtfully to questions raised as we read *The Kite Runner*. Blogs also gave them more time and space to think through their answers than responding in class did. Peer responses to their posts also helped build community in the class as students got to know one another on a deeper level than through class time alone. And in an eSchoolNews article, a Pew Internet survey reported that blogging helped teens become more prolific writers and more teen bloggers "believe that writing is essential to later success in life" as compared to students who don't blog (eSchoolNews Staff and Wire Service Reports 2008). Our students see blogging as another avenue for publication and writing, and we can build on this medium in ways that help develop their literacy skills while teaching critical literacies for keeping them safe and helping them understand issues of privacy.

Teachers with class blogs can use the common space of a class community blog to help students understand the affordances of blogging in humorous ways as well. On the blog A really different place (http://areallydifferentplace .org), April awards, such as Best Overall Blogger, Most Humorous Blog Post, and Most Controversial Post, were given out for student blogs. To the left of the classroom blog is a list of student blogs so visitors can see all the student blogs, thereby increasing readership and underscoring the award recipients (you can see why Clara won Best Overall and Most Controversial post, for example). The student blogs are extensive and well written and contain comments by peers as well as visitors to the site—fairly impressive, especially when you realize that the writers of posts like "Inaugural Addresses: Obama vs. Truman" are sixth graders.

Overall, blogs are one of the most established technologies being used to read and write on the Web today. Many of our students are already familiar with the idea of writing about themselves, their thoughts, and their lives online, and many find it motivating and engaging. There are safe ways to use blogs with a class project, to organize a class community, and to support individual students as writers and thinkers. Moreover, blogs can be set up through free sites, monitored by you as the teacher, and shared with the community. Students can learn how to read and write more critically, understand issues of privacy, construct multimedia texts, create individual spaces that support their own learning, and reflect on their development as readers, writers, and thinkers. Blogs are a good way to get started, as I hope these examples have shown. You can find more examples in the appendix at the end of the book.

Wikis

Wikis, on the other hand, are easier used as information resources rather than sites for publication. The wiki (from the Hawaiian word *wiki wiki*, meaning "quick") was designed to be a fast, easy-to-use online resource for information. The wiki you are probably most familiar with, Wikipedia, is the largest and most complex wiki of its kind. Of course, there has been a long debate about the validity of Wikipedia because as well as being an information storing house, Wikipedia is an open-source site that allows anyone who creates a username to add to or edit the entries. This type of perceived free-for-all can be worrisome, but Wikipedia employs legions of editors, mostly unpaid, who take responsibility for entries and regularly police them for inaccuracies. Some studies have found the perceived credibility of Wikipedia to be extremely high, even higher in some cases than traditionally published articles (Chesney 2006), but whether you allow students to use Wikipedia as a resource or just a place to get started (the links and outside resources at the bottom of every Wikipedia entry are an excellent place to get good sites for research and information), the idea of a collaborative site for information is growing.

Using a wiki with students gives you an easy way to create a site with multiple pages of content you can either control or allow students to add to. Free sites such as PBworks (www.pbworks.com) and Wikispaces (www.wikispaces.com), provide free wiki templates; creating the content is as easy as typing on a word processor: just click to edit and follow the guidelines and tools you have available. The interface looks much like Microsoft Word, so the tools and buttons are familiar to anyone who uses that program. (See Chapter 4 for more on creating your own wiki.) If you want to create a wiki on a project or unit—Shakespeare, the Harlem Renaissance, or just about anything—a wiki provides you with a front page that is easy to add links to for additional pages where you can collect online resources, upload files for students to read, and so forth. Students can also have group pages where they can upload resources for papers, projects, and presentations.

As the author of the wiki you retain control over who can read it, add to it, and edit it, and students who have access to the Internet can get to the page from any online computer and visit the links, at school, from home, or other locations—just as with a blog. Wikis are useful for creating a space to collect links, files, and other information; for creating a space for students to upload information and collaborate on projects; for creating an ongoing online space that can be used over and over again; and for getting good resources to students whose own research may not take them to the sites you want them to visit. Perhaps most important, wikis build on collaboration—they grow over time through the collective wisdom gained when learning about the topic or project. This is the kind of learning and work our students will need to be successful in higher education and beyond as the world places more value on collaboration, especially across long geographic distances. Through a wiki, your students can work together with other students anywhere in the world—in English or by learning other languages, by posting and watching videos, by reading and visiting online sites, and so on.

If you're getting the sense that blogs and wikis allow for new types of texts and publishing, you're absolutely right. As with blogs, the audience for a wiki can be anyone in the world, or it can be restricted to an audience of your choosing. Either way, deciding to publish or save the information and make the wiki—and the blog—"live" constitutes publication. You and your students can see your work as part of the World Wide Web—a heady, inspiring experience. Allowing students to contribute sites and information to a class wiki builds on their expertise too, giving them a voice and an incentive to continue participating. Rather than a paper packet of articles or a list of links, a wiki is a vibrant resource that can and does change through use. Like a blog, its story is told day by day in how it is used and modified.

Wikis are newer to education, but their use is taking off, especially through sites such as Wikis in Education (http://wikisineducation.wetpaint.com). As with blogs, the easiest way to begin is by creating a class wiki that will continue to expand as your class does different projects and needs to add different resources from the Web and student work, make connections within your district, and so on. Wikis are basically a way to develop a project base of information on the Web by creating a main page and offering a list of links that can be added to infinitely. As the teacher, you can opt to be the only one to add resources, or you can choose to share that capability with students, other teachers, or even parents and other members of the community. As the original creator, you have control over what eventually appears (more on this in Chapter 5), so you retain ultimate editorial control.

Classroom wikis can be used to list assignments, house classroom resources used to learn more about the topics you are studying, create study guides, and keep parents informed about what's going on in class. In her grade 5 classroom wiki (http://mpolselli.wetpaint.com/?t=anon), Mrs. Polselli keeps parents informed of what is going on in her classroom; offers links to upcoming events such as the 2009 school poetry slam; and includes her open house PowerPoint, syllabus, study guides, announcements, and more. She also has links to websites by authors the students are reading, including Jerry Spinelli, and webquests on books such as *Maniac Magee*. Her classroom wiki serves as an extension of the class by providing students and parents with resources not just to keep track of what the students are doing in class, but to extend what they can do beyond the classroom. This is exactly the strength of using a class wiki: you can expand student learning and invite parent participation by building on these resources.

Another type of wiki particularly suited for teens is a group project format or teen-created wiki. Because wikis group online resources in such a way that they can be accessed by anyone with an Internet connection, a group of students can use them to do research and compile project references easily and then publish those references online. In a way, this direct publication of resources online can also be used to circumvent the issue of plagiarism, since it is very clear where the information the students are using came from. A wiki by two students on Civil War and Revolutionary Women Soldiers (http://victoriaaurorahistoryfairproject.wetpaint.com) profiles women who fought in the Revolutionary and Civil Wars; the wiki was created as part of their entry into a history fair project and includes profiles of many women soldiers, as well as photos and includes the recurring question, "So why do we not learn about them in our textbooks?" Good question. The resources the students used for the project are clearly delineated as links in the wiki, so no confusion arises about how they got their information.

Other student wikis help address current issues and raise awareness, building on the ability of a wiki to publish important information to a large audience. One such example is the wiki How to Help Save Darfur (http://savedarfurnhs.wetpaint.com) from North Hampton School in North Hampton, New Hampshire. This wiki, which was nominated for a wiki award, raises awareness about the genocide in Darfur while listing information about how site visitors can help. A link lists a letter that the eighth graders who wrote the site sent to local newspapers and newsletters and a reply from a local congressional representative in response to a letter the students sent her. This wiki represents the research the students did in response to a crucial problem in our world, as well as how they used this new technology and its literacies to address that problem.

And finally, wikis are a great way to share resources and create community between teachers and others in the field of education. Teacher/peer wikis collect resources that can be shared between teachers, schools, and communities around the world. Some exist as social networking sites for teachers to communicate different ideas and teaching tools, some demonstrate techniques and technologies, and some are specific to curriculum themes, such as the Teachers College Writers and Readers Workshop Model (http://writersrock .wetpaint.com) or literacy centers in the classroom (http://literacycenters .wetpaint.com).

At the wiki Welcome to Learning the Wiki Way (http://learning2shanghai .wetpaint.com), Jason Welker uses the wiki itself to introduce teachers to using a wiki for instructional purposes. His wiki is well constructed and easy to understand, with links on the sidebar devoted to resource sharing, student-created content, course evaluations, learning and assessing the wiki, exam review, and so on. While the wiki is geared toward university learning, many, if not most, of the ideas can be used with high school and even middle school students.

At Bud the Teacher's Wiki (http://budtheteacher.com/wiki/), Bud the Teacher, a prolific blogger and technology integrator, has created a massive wiki with tons of resources and links to other teacher blogs and wikis. He includes a Student Blogging Handbook, Writing Project Blogs, a link to his Telling Stories with Technology project on digital storytelling, and examples of letters he has sent home to parents to explain technology projects including blogging. He includes links to his presentation "The Compleatly Connected Teacher" at the National Council of Teachers of English Convention 2006, which includes samples of students' writing.

Wikis are so expansive and so simple that they can contain almost anything you can think of. They can be used for classroom information, group work, student projects, community outreach, teacher/peer community projects, teacher resources, and much more. They can be accessed from anywhere and added to infinitely, whether by you alone or by anyone involved in the project. Their simplicity and expansiveness give them a particular power that makes them useful in many situations and an excellent first technology to try on in your classroom.

Digital Stories

One way to think of changes in reading, writing, and publication in digital spaces is to understand that we now have many different venues and tools for telling stories and providing information. We can communicate immediately or over time; we can write out what we mean and craft formal language, or use immediate abbreviations in order to save time. We can tell a story in words that need to be read; give information through an annotated list of links that can be visited; interact and create an ongoing story through a blog and its comments. We can even create and publish digital stories using visual means—including still images, video, music, and voice. These digital stories involve writing and publishing too, and they can be the hook you need to get the most reluctant student in your class to create a story he or she is deeply invested in by making it the best that it can be.

By definition, digital stories are stories that are created by using visual modes—like still images or video. Like written texts, they have a beginning, a middle, and an end, move along a conventional arc, introduce characters, and have a setting. In fact, the best digital stories are planned and scripted well in advance through the use of storyboards, scripts, collections of images, and more (I will go into more depth about how to create a digital story in Chapter 5).

The beginnings of digital storytelling are usually traced to the Center for Digital Storytelling (www.storycenter.org) in Berkeley, California. The Center has been using digital stories created from narratives using still images, written scripts or stories, and video or music for the last fifteen years in collaboration with schools, communities, and other diverse groups. Their original Digital

Storytelling Workshop is still the model used by many for teaching digital storytelling, and you can find their Digital Storytelling Cookbook online at www.storycenter.org.cookbook.html (the first two chapters can be viewed for free and the entire cookbook is available for purchase online). Through their site you can view a wide variety of stories from adults and teens organized by themes including community, education, family, identity, health, and place. Their storytelling projects have been used to profile issues with health care, social work and the foster care system, gender and justice in South Africa, and immigrant workers' rights, to name a few. Through the Center, digital stories have been a powerful medium to bring voice and image to disenfranchised, silent, or overlooked groups and issues.

Using digital images and computer technologies can be an excellent way to get a student writing, particularly a reluctant student. While many of us require creative writing from our students and even, on occasion, allow them to illustrate it, most of the creative writing in schools is words on paper shown to the teacher alone. On the other hand, asking students to script and storyboard a film and then create it can engage them because it gives them a larger audience (you can have a film festival of sorts where students show their films to the class as well as post it online to a class wiki or blog) and a vested interest in the creation of the story. Also, the higher-order thinking required in order to create a digital story is complex and sophisticated. Whether students are using digital still images or shooting live video, they have to be aware of how the visual element tells the story they want to tell—how it matches the words and the overall scope of the story. In addition, music, voice-overs, and other elements can be layered into the story, further deepening the meaning and the decisions students have to make.

Digital stories have been used by groups of students throughout the country and the world to tell true and fictional tales, raise awareness about important public issues in the form of public announcements, and so forth. Students express great interest in making digital stories, and not only because they will be shown to others. In a world where collaboration and creativity are increasingly valued, digital stories push students to script, shoot, edit, and produce something that feels important to them. We know from years of research that students learn best by doing, and the creation of a project that is wholly their own is motivating, interesting, challenging, and engaging. Digital stories are creations that push our students to go beyond writing a single-draft story; in order to complete a digital story, our students must be able to plan out the arc of the narrative, fit characters and setting with visual elements, and add voice and narration. With the advent of YouTube and TeacherTube, digital video has become a much larger part of the Internet and one that our students are familiar with. Many of our students already know how to create and post video, sometimes of a sort that should not be posted online. Through creating and working on a school-based digital video, we can open up the conversation as to what is appropriate to post online, what isn't, and why.

More and more schools are beginning to use digital stories as another way to engage students in creating narratives and learning story structure and grammar. Those elements essential to any story—setting, characters, and plot structure—are just as important in a digital story because they help the audience make sense of the images, sound, and text. Many teachers design digital story projects to help groups of students understand the uses of writing across a variety of genres as well—from narrative to persuasive and informational. Digital stories can be fictional or informational, such as public service announcements. They can persuade an audience on an issue or move them to reach out and act in particular ways to help specific communities.

At the Wisdom Lost, Wisdom Found wiki (http://wisdomlostwisdom found.wikispaces.com/introduction), students have created digital stories based on the oral histories of local community members from other generations. Students created interview questions and chose both video and still images taken from selected sites within their city. They interviewed four people and created a digital story that wove together the information they gathered from each of the interviews. The story told how profiling members and visiting the spaces of their community helped them view it differently.

At the Electronic Pencil, a sixth-grade writing workshop weblog (http://epencil.edublogs.org), students' digital stories are embedded into the class blog and run the gamut from a rap based on Quidditch from the Harry Potter movies to animated movies based on the idea of personification. These movies are actually still images from the Flickr photo-sharing site of student computer drawings with titles that play somewhat like a slide show—showing that there are a variety of ways that students and teachers can create and post digital stories and use this medium throughout the process of teaching and learning.

Other teachers and schools have used digital stories for everything from classroom management to participation in larger projects, such as StoryCorps and PBS Multimedia Storytelling. An excellent site with links to these and other examples of digital storytelling sites, including good websites with how-to tips, can be found at: http://electronicportfolios.com/digitalstory/index.html. On this site, for example, is a link to a teacher information page on PBS.org (www.pbs.org/americanfamily/teacher3.html) that gives excellent tips on a digital storytelling project for teachers and students and that includes a storyboarding handout, links to national standards, and has detailed procedural tips. *Edutopia*, the educational technology magazine for K–12 educators sponsored by the George Lucas Foundation (and an excellent resource on educational technology in its own right), offers tips and information in an online article on how to use digital storytelling in your classroom (www.edutopia.org/use -digital-storytelling-classroom). And finally, Classroom 2.0, a Ning or online social network for teachers interested in Web 2.0 applications in the classroom, has a separate focus area for teachers interested in using digital storytelling in the classroom (www.classroom20.com/group/digitalstorytelling).

Whether you choose to use digital stories for creative writing, persuasive pieces, historical or social studies projects, or some combination, this tool is an excellent way to motivate and engage students in the process of constructing a multimedia narrative as well as learning research skills, writing, and scripting. Digital storytelling is a form of writing as much as it is a technological creation—and learning to author using new forms of media is only going to become more important as new tools become more prevalent. Also, digital storytelling is built on the same framework as more traditional written forms—in order for a digital story, whether fictional, historical, persuasive, or another genre, to succeed, it must have the same components as the written version, must make sense to the viewer, and must work through to a logical conclusion. Digital stories are just a powerful way to marry new media to long-valued genres and ways of making meaning of the world—and our students can learn a great deal from this marriage.

Conclusion

Blogs, wikis, and digital stories are just three means of using digital tools to support new literacies in the classroom. There are many others—but these are three that represent a good starting place. They range from simple processes, like starting up a classroom blog, to more complex tools, like creating student group digital stories. They make use of free, online sites like Blogger and PBworks as well as the Center for Digital Storytelling. They allow for a range of practices—creative writing, research, information presentation. Most important, they can be done with a lot of technology or just a little—and there are examples from all over to the world. In the next chapter, I show you how you can set up and use these tools in your classroom.

The Nuts and Bolts of Creating and Using Blogs, Wikis, and Digital Stories in Your Classroom

4

Since this book focuses on teaching literacy through using blogs, wikis, and digital stories, this chapter serves as a how-to manual for setting up and using these tools with free resources available online. Whether you want to try creating a class blog, have students create blogs of their own, put together a class or project wiki, or implement a digital storytelling project, this chapter lists resources for each. It is possible to use free online resources to blog, create a wiki, and present digital stories, and there are many more inexpensive options. If some are blocked by firewall software at your school or in your district, other educational versions of these free sites probably will not be. (In my experience, explaining the scope and intent of a supervised project using a blocked site is a good way to get the site unblocked for your use by your technology coordinator.)

In terms of consents and permissions, most schools and districts have parents and/or students sign technology fair use forms at the beginning of the year that will also cover technology projects you implement in your own classroom. If you would like to create a consent form that is particular to the project you are doing, Will Richardson, whose site, Weblogg-Ed (http:// weblogg-ed.com/), is an excellent resource for all things technological in terms of education, has good consent form examples in his book *Blogs, Wikis, Podcasts, and Other Powerful Tools for the Classroom* (2006). In fact, his book is another fantastic resource for understanding and using blogs, wikis, and podcasts in education at all levels and across multiple content areas.

It's also important to keep in mind that you don't need to have a computer lab available—or laptops for every student—to use many of these tools. You can set up a classroom blog or wiki that students can access at home or from the library; you can use groups on a couple of computers to do digital stories, and you can make use of free online sites and software that comes with many computers.

What, Exactly, Are the Parts of a Blog? What Do I Need to Know?

First, let's go more in depth into the components of a blog. As mentioned in Chapter 3, a blog is a website that is authored by a single person or a group of people. The main text in a blog is called a post, and it is put up or published in reverse order, meaning that the most recent posts show up first and a reader can scroll through them to read older posts (most blogs don't put all the posts on the main page after you reach a certain number but do have a button or link called "older posts" or "archives"). The post can be any length—that's one of the strengths of a hypertext—and can incorporate visual elements like photos, links to other information online, and links to videos. Posting is easy; you just type in the space provided just as you would with most word processors. Most free blogging sites have buttons at the top of the post screen that allow you to use italics, bold, add a link, and more.

With each post usually comes the opportunity to comment (although this feature can be disabled if you choose). The ability to comment is an important feature of a blog because it allows the blog to become a multiauthored text whose meaning changes through the interplay of the main posts and the comments. Commenting also keeps a blog author aware of audience—even if only a few comments are made, this represents tangible evidence that the blog is being read. Authors can write posts that they want commented on by asking questions or giving readers links to something the author wants reactions to.

Blogs can be given any title you like, and they have their own particular URL, making them a site unto themselves that can be posted as a link on another site, sent out in an email, and shared through other means. When a post is published, it is then viewable by anyone who has the blog URL (you can also set privacy parameters so that readers must have a password to view the blog). Comments must be added to the particular post to which they refer; that is, I read something you wrote and then I click on the comment link at the bottom of the post, which usually requires the name of the person commenting and an email address. Students and authors need not use their full names or even real names; many teachers have students set up a free Gmail (Google email account) and use a first name plus a last initial or a pseudonym when posting. As long as you know who your students are, there's no reason for them to use their real names online, especially if you have concerns about identity theft (although I have yet to see any cases of this in my own use of blogs or in that of any of the teachers I have spoken with).

How Do I Create a Blog?

There are several online, free sources for creating blogs. I have been using blogs with my students since 2005 and have yet had to pay for the service. There are subscription services, but mostly they offer prettier, more sophisticated layouts rather than different, more important features. The best-known, most-used free service is Blogger (www.blogger.com). As of this writing, Blogger was hosting millions of blogs, and thousands more are being created every day. Blogger is now owned by Google, making it fairly stable and easy to use. Literally anyone who has something to say can create a blog—something that is important to point out to students as they create their own blogs to do research or use or contribute to a class blog.

On Blogger, a user needs a Gmail account, also available for free, and a title for the blog. The blog will be assigned a unique URL that will locate it on the Internet for others to see (although it can also be set to only be seen by friends or invitees). There are a range of layouts a user can choose that give the blog color and style. Another free service, used by many in the educational community—especially if Blogger is blocked in their school district—is Edublogs.com. Again, although there also are subscription options, I have found the free options to be more than sufficient. I use Blogger because I have found it easier to use, but both sites easily fit the bill as free sites that offer users a way to quickly set up a free blog. Once the blog is set up, the user simply has to go back, log in to either Blogger or Edublogs, and click to write a new post. As mentioned before, writing a post is easy because the screen looks much like any other word processing screen. Posts have titles that give readers a quick sense of what the post is about; this is also a way to teach a manner of summarizing—What would you title this post to communicate its essence and also pique the reader's interest?

Readers of blogs have to enter in the blog's URL; I usually create a page on a course Web page or wiki (more on setting up wikis later in this chapter) with links to all the students' blogs. They can then read the posts and reply by clicking on the word *comments* at the end of that post. A new screen pops up that looks like a smaller version of the post screen. The comments screen requires the reader to log in using an email address so comments can't be anonymous—this is important so that students understand they can't make inappropriate comments because their email address is attached to any comment they make. This is where the Gmail account comes in handy as well—they don't have to attach their entire name to their Gmail account or to their blog. In fact, I tell them to only use their first name and last initial, and I keep a list of their Gmail accounts with their full names so I know whose blogs and comments belong to whom and I can keep track. This protects their privacy online while still allowing me to create accountability. In addition, since blogs are public, parents, other teachers, and even administrators may be invited to read what students have been writing about a particular topic. I have found mentioning this to students to be particularly helpful with accountability as well as with helping them take their writing and thinking up to another level. Regardless of whether you use Blogger.com, Edublogs, or another free blogging site, you and your students can easily set up blogs and use them to support writing, reading, thinking, and literacy in your classroom.

So How Do I Blog with My Students? How Do I Integrate Blogging into My Teaching?

Blogging in the classroom usually entails one of three setups:

1. You can set up a class blog where students contribute to one main blog and comment on one another's entries.

2. You can set up a blog of your own to keep students and parents informed about the class, put out syllabi and assignment descriptions, and use it as a clearinghouse for information on your class.

3. You and your students can each set up a blog to use individually.

Often teachers begin with the second kind of blog, a class blog, because it is easy to conceptualize and set up, and it gets parents and students into the habit of going to an online site as part of the class routine and learning experience. I have used blogs this way in the past (as have many others; see Chapter 3). One of the strengths of the class blog is that it is easy to control since you, as the teacher, put up the information you want. You can even control the comments by turning them off or on. A class information blog is a great way to keep parents in the loop and even to ask them to contribute to class projects and themes in their children's learning.

Will Richardson writes about using classroom blogs as both a "class portal" that gives a view to parents and others of what the class is doing and an "online filing cabinet" where students can get copies of syllabi, assignments, and any other papers handed out in class. He points out that making these files available online cuts way down on the number of students who can claim they couldn't do the assignment because they lost the assignment sheet. That's another strength of a blog—it is available to anyone with a connection to the Internet (although you can password-protect it, which will be discussed later in this chapter) regardless of platform or computer. Overall, a class blog set up to support and reflect the running of a class is easy to create and maintain, and it does much of the important work of keeping students, parents, and administration in the loop. With these new technologies, transparency is becoming easier and more important—students must take responsibility for checking class blogs for updates about classes and homework assignments, among other things.

The next, most logical step in incorporating a blog into a classroom is to create a collaborative class blog. This is a blog that allows both you and the students to make the original posts to the blog. This particular format is very useful in supporting student writing as a class, since anything they post in the main part of the blog is read by their peers and can be commented on. For example, if students are working on five-paragraph persuasive essays, each student can post a draft to the blog (you might want to stagger how many students you have posting drafts so you don't have twenty-five all at once). Other students can then read the draft and add comments concerning format, content, mechanics, and more. Students don't all have to post a full draft, nor do they have to post at the same time. In order to stagger posts, you can put students into publishing groups and have members from each group post when their group publication date comes up. Regardless of how many students post a draft, all other classmates as well as the teacher can comment on it. This is a great, concrete way to teach peer editing and review. You can post a sample comment, encourage students to follow your example, and draw out short comments by responding to them.

Class blogs can be used in other ways besides posting drafts of writing. One common and powerful way is responding to reading a novel or short story. A great example of this is the blog Will Richardson describes in a Modern American Literature class in response to the book *The Secret Life of Bees*, which is featured in Richardson's book on blogs, wikis, and podcasts. The teacher's students created an online guide to the book, posting responses to each of the chapters along with a link for comments (which they changed from "comments" to "discuss"). Students in the class could read the study guide for each chapter, which outlined the themes of the chapter as well as how specific instances in the chapter related to the book overall. For example, in the post on themes for chapters 9 and 10, some students wrote: "The themes for chapters 9 and 10 would most closely be compared to that of realization. Realization can be in many different degrees and is not always looked at as a theme. Realization does change a person's perspective which can brighten or dim the mood of the entire book and chapters 9 and 10 have a large amount of that." Students could respond to this or any other chapter post. In addition, the teacher created a space on the blog where students could post their overall impressions of the book once they finished reading it. All posts are available for other students to read, thereby increasing the audience and creating a tangible conversation.

Most interestingly, the author of *The Secret Life of Bees*, Sue Monk Kidd, learned about the class book blog and stopped by to answer student questions. The teacher posted a list of ten questions raised by the students, which Monk Kidd responded to, but first she wrote:

Dear Students,

It is an exceptionally nice honor to have you reading my novel in your Modern American Literature class! I'm extremely impressed with your weblog, which I've been following. What fun for the author to listen in on your discussions and see the wonderful and provocative artistic interpretations that you've created. The experience has opened my eyes to new ideas about my own work!

The author went on to describe her experiences as a student in her high school English classes and when she decided she wanted to be an author. These kinds of interactions, in which the author of a book can respond to student questions and connect with the ideas students raise about the reading of a novel, are few and far between. Writing to a blog, however, allows students and teachers to publish their ideas and make them available to the world at large, including the authors of the books they read. As well, Monk Kidd's long response to the students' questions gave them another text they can refer back to in their study of writing, thinking, and learning about how an author crafts a novel, the decisions she or he makes, and why. The experience of reading a book is enriched far beyond the classroom walls to potentially incorporate students in other classes worldwide, alternate teachers, parents, and even authors. In addition, the blog can link to an author's Web page, other resources about the book, and in this case, information and reviews on the film version of the novel.

All in all, whether you use a blog as a classroom website and online repository, a classroom conversation and interaction, or individual student avenues for writing and publication, it can serve a range of text types that can energize students to read, write, and think more deeply. Blogs document learning, push students to think through writing, offer opportunities for reflection, create communities, and much more. They can be created for free and set with varying levels of authorship and privacy. Blogs are a tool well worth exploring for a variety of purposes in classrooms from upper elementary through higher education.

But what if you need a space simply to publish information, not focus on writing? What if you want a free, easy-to-set-up clearinghouse for resources and ideas? What if you want and need an easy, online means to support students working on a group project? Then perhaps what you need is a wiki.

How Does a Wiki Differ from a Blog? When Would I Use One Rather Than the Other?

In contrast to blogs, a wiki is another type of Web space that focuses on allowing you to host or put up information, often for free. Unlike a blog, a wiki is not usually characterized by a single author who is writing over a course of time but rather a group of people who are contributing to a source of knowledge. The best-known example, discussed in Chapter 3, is Wikipedia—an online encyclopedia available in hundreds of languages that can be edited by anyone who signs up and becomes a member. This collaborative aspect, along with the ability to quickly update information, is the key to a wiki. Users and authors of a wiki can quickly put up information. Since they have to log in to do so, a trail exists as to who posted what information, and a wiki's owners and editors have the ultimate ability to decide what information to keep and what to jettison. Therefore, the users and authors of a wiki learn to create and collaborate on information, an important skill in a world where collaboration and creation, especially concerning technology, is increasingly important. Tapscott and Williams (2006) write, in *Wikinomics*, that more and more business models require the ability to collaborate across sites to get information to sources quickly, check on the veracity of information, and create new business models. A wiki is a perfect example of a tool that teaches collaboration.

The components of a wiki are simple. Each wiki begins with a home or main page composed of links to additional pages. This home page can be added to continually; there is no limit to the number of pages a wiki may contain. Most wikis, with the exception of those intended to be encyclopedic, are centered on a topic or project and act as clearinghouses of information. A wiki can be created by a teacher and added to by that teacher alone, the teacher and students or other members of an educational community such as parents or administrators, or solely the students. A wiki can be accessed by anyone who has an Internet connection, regardless of the type of computer, and does not have to be accessed at school. It can also be made private, to be accessed via password only. Because wikis are usually set up around information, you may not have the same privacy concerns as with a blog, and they can be used as resources for other classes. And because wikis are published to the Web,

they can be open to people from all over the world and can act as collaborative projects between classrooms, schools, and even countries.

From the main page, links are set up that connect to new pages. These
new pages may be lists of links themselves: resources for a particular project,
or typed information about something like a class assignment, upcoming field
trip, or preparation for state exams. As noted earlier, the number of pages that
hook to the main page is infinite, and the form these pages can take ranges
from lists of links, to static, typed information, to embedded educational video
and historical photographs, to links to educational sites, and much more. The
links can be open to editing if you choose to share the password with students, parents, or faculty, or they just can be available for read-only viewing if
you decide not to share the password. Many wikis include the host email
address on each page; interested users can email the host for a password to
add to the page or send content they think should be added. As with a blog, a
teacher can assert a measure of control over the authorship of a wiki and the
range of audience—from students to parents, fellow teachers, administration,
and others. Many teachers interested in using wikis in their classrooms search
out other examples and visit classroom wikis, so your wiki may very well end
up as a good model for other teachers interested in trying it themselves.

How Do I Set Up and Use a Wiki?

There are free sites that will allow you to set up and use a wiki. They have pay-
ing options but in my experience, the free options work very well and, like
blogs, I have yet to pay to host a wiki in the three years I have been using
them in my teaching. I use PBworks (www.pbworks.com)—the *PB* stands for
"peanut butter," their idea being that using a wiki is as easy as making a
peanut butter sandwich. You create an account on the site and then you are
ready to create your first wiki, beginning with the home page. The nice thing
about PBworks is that it includes templates for educational wikis (one of the
questions they ask you when you set up your wiki is what use you plan for
it—if you choose educational, they load templates for syllabus, group project,
etc.). Even without the templates, creating pages is easy because each page is
set up to closely resemble that of using a word processor. Other free wiki sites

include Wikispaces (www.wikispaces.com) and Wikis in Education at Wetpaint.com (http://wikisineducation.wetpaint.com).

A wiki can be used as a warehouse for a classroom to post information throughout the year, as a project site for a particular class project, or as a central location for students working on a class project. Teachers have created wikis to keep students informed by posting assignments and links to good resources. They have additionally created wikis to support class projects on writing about topics such as the Holocaust, learning to write in particular genres such as persuasive writing, and reading particular types of fiction such as poetry or short stories. Instead of sending students out to search the Web endlessly for good sites, they can go to a wiki that holds links to the sites a teacher has already vetted. These links can stay up for as long as the teacher chooses, so they can be used by other classes or in following semesters.

Perhaps the easiest wiki to begin with is a class wiki that is used to hold paperwork, class assignments, and the class calendar. The front or home page of the wiki can list information about the class and links to each of the topic headings available in the wiki—each link will lead to a page with a class assignment, description of an upcoming project, a class calendar (PBworks has free, downloadable calendars that can be placed within their pages, for example), and links to other class wikis or home pages with similar resources.

> Because wikis are published to the Web, they can be open to others from all over the world and can act as collaborative projects between classrooms, schools, and even countries.

Another easy-to-conceptualize wiki can center around a project topic or theme—a genre of writing, a period of history, or a type of resource. Given all the information available online, a wiki can easily be built to cut through the time and energy needed to find helpful resources. For instance, a standardized writing assessment might call on students to use primary historical documents as sources. Students often have difficulties first understanding the differences between primary and secondary sources and then finding them. A wiki on writing with primary sources might include pages that define primary and secondary sources, links to good writing examples using primary sources, and links to excellent repositories where primary source materials may be found, such as the Library of Congress website (www.loc.gov/index.html). Or, if students are working on narratives based on the Holocaust, but you want to steer them toward valuable sites while limiting their exposure to some of the more explicit and disturbing materials available online, you might build a project wiki whose links list those sites you have visited and vetted ahead of time.

Creating a project wiki for research purposes does take time up front—not in terms of computer expertise (most of the computer work takes place in terms of cutting and pasting URLs) but rather in terms of finding sites you deem useful and appropriate. Yet the effort pays off by giving your students concrete lists of sites they can use and cutting down on their search time and frustration when looking for useful information. As with the class wiki, project wikis can be used over again in following semesters or with other classes, so this work will always be available as long as the site links remain active. In addition, students can create wikis themselves, especially when working in groups on projects. This allows you, as a teacher, to see the resources they have put together directly without having to go through a bibliography. A project wiki also puts together in one space all the materials students need for a presentation, written paper, or other assessment. Overall, wikis provide an excellent space for collaborative work, resource management, and classroom communication. A wiki can be expanded even further than a blog, so it may be a better choice for a classroom website when you know your students will be doing multiple projects. And the flexibility of being able to create what is essentially a limitless website is invaluable.

What Is a Digital Story? How Do Digital Stories Work?

A digital story is a multimedia story that is built from a compilation of digital still images and/or video, with text, audio, music, and narrative. These stories begin with a written or composed plan—from a storyboard or web to a fully written script—and are then edited by adding images, video, and music. Ohler (2007), in *Digital Storytelling in the Classroom: New Media Pathways to Literacy, Learning, and Creativity*, states that "digital storytelling uses personal digital technology to combine a number of media into a coherent narrative" (15).

Digital stories are all around us, he points out, first, because stories are one of the main ways we make sense of the world and second, because digital media often use narrative components such as visual means and story grammar. Think of online videos on YouTube, personal stories using video and images on blogs, or stories told through images and comments on photo sites like Flickr. Ohler explains that, for our students, "Digital is the language they speak, media is the environment in which they feel comfortable, and the multimedia collage is the new global language" (11). That fits well with the goals of the literacy classroom, in that stories and the components of narrative such as setting, characters, problems and resolutions, and climax are our purview. Our students also learn well through the frame of narrative, as Jerome Bruner pointed out years ago. We construct learning often by viewing it through the lens of story. Much of what we teach, in terms of content and structure, about language and particular periods of writing and history is or can be taught by constructing it as a story. Digital stories are the new literacies version of that, a fresh practice that builds on the affordances of original tools and media that let us and our students tell our stories differently and more widely than ever before. Again, this process results in motivating and engaging those students least likely to enjoy learning in the literacy classroom.

A digital story works to build on a story narrative using new media. Students create a narrative, first using traditional tools—a rough plan using a web or storyboard, then a more polished script. Depending on the focus of the story, students do research, conduct interviews, and gather video and still images. I use the plural term *students* because a digital story project is a large, complex task that lends itself well to collaboration, especially when each student has a particular task and is accountable not only for the entire project but for specific pieces, and so must report out on two levels—how the story is coming along more generally, and how each student is doing in his or her particular job.

The first stages of any digital story project are crucial. No digital story will be successful if students don't first complete a rough plan and then a script, both of which you can sign off on before allowing them to begin collecting images or video. These initial pieces allow the project to blend traditional and new literacies and provide an essential foundation for a complete digital story, one that will have the necessary elements for any good story, not just a digital one. Once students have a plan in hand, you and they can decide what kinds of media best fit the story they want to tell.

A digital story does not have to involve video per se. Many digital stories are created using digital still photos—the editing is the same. Both video and still images are integrated and edited using basic software such as iMovie, which is standard on any Mac purchased within the last few years, or MovieMaker, which comes with most PCs. Both software programs are fairly easy to install if not already on your computer, easy to use, and have extensive tutorials and help sections, and students pick them up very quickly, in my experience. In fact, with digital stories, the students usually have less trouble with the technology than with creating and sustaining the narrative to make a really good story—which is, after all, the lesson we want them to walk away with.

Say, for example, you want students to create a persuasive digital story—a story convincing their audience to recycle, reject student uniforms, or stop smoking. Students write persuasive pieces throughout the grade levels; having them create a persuasive digital story is just another way to teach the rhetoric of persuasion while also teaching them essential critical media literacy: the ability to take apart and understand the components of digital media and understand how they work together to persuade and impart a particular message. As Ohler writes, "Most important, the media production process requires students to synthesize imagination, creativity, research, and critical thinking in order to translate their ideas into some form of media-based expression" (2007, 11). In order to create their persuasive story, students must choose their topic and research facts and evidence to support their points. They would have to write a script or create a storyboard, film video or collect still images, and either add a voice-over or words to the film. Then students edit the images or film together into a digital story that persuades their audience and is true to the evidence and research they collected.

When Might I Want to Use Digital Stories with My Students?

Digital stories are a wonderful option when you want your students to create a nontraditional narrative that will nonetheless require scripting and all the traditional components of a narrative; create a group project that has many layers and opportunities for participation; or work on an interdisciplinary project that spans multiple content areas. All that is needed are computers with editing software (iMovie comes free with most Apple laptops and MovieMaker is available on most PCs), digital images—which can be still images, so you don't necessarily have to use video—and recording capabilities. For less than $50, you can purchase digital voice recorders or just use the recording software built into the computers you will be using.

In one recent project I worked on in East Orange, New Jersey, students from both an eighth- and a fifth-grade class worked together to interview members of their community about what East Orange was like during the Depression years (the topic they were studying in history at the time as well as a salient topic given the recession going on at the time). Groups of students found images of East Orange online from that time period; others wrote scripts and researched questions to ask participants. Teams of students from both classrooms went out and interviewed community members, others recorded voice-overs to stitch together the digital story, while still others worked on putting together all the materials into digital movies. Every student from both classes participated in the project and, when I visited, all indicated that they liked and even preferred learning history this way because it was more hands-on and they got to learn directly from the people who experienced it.

These kinds of projects may seem daunting, but once you break them down into their components, they are feasible. Often the students know the technology better than we do and so, as teachers, we work to help them with the research and questioning, keeping the project on track academically. There are many different centers, such as the Center for Digital Storytelling, which offer steps and guidelines (http://centerfordigitalstorytelling.org). An excellent book for those new to digital storytelling as well as for those who would like to know more about it is Jason Ohler's *Digital Storytelling in the Classroom* (2007) mentioned previously. He also has an excellent website (http://jasonohler.com) with articles, resources, and keynote addresses to get you excited about digital storytelling.

I have seen this technique work in my own classes, particularly with those students who are least engaged in the writing and reading classroom. Digital storytelling offers them a way to read and write differently, which is crucial if we want to see them become absorbed in what we are doing and begin to see literacy as essential. And certainly this is true, too, of blogging and wikis. These new technologies can be the perfect way to reach out and capture students like Vinnie, who slip so easily from our grasp.

5

Using Technology to Address Ten Key Issues in Reading and Writing Instruction

This chapter outlines the ten key ways in which blogs, digital stories, and wikis work to help students in the literacy classroom be more interested, improve their writing, increase their engagement with content, and much more. These themes represent important issues that all literacy teachers struggle with in their classrooms along with ideas and tips on how these digital tools can help address these points for you and your students. New literacies, as I have discussed throughout the book, are simply the interaction between literacy practices like reading and writing and new tools—and when these new tools are used to good purpose, they can foster creative and deep literacy learning.

Safety

Students need to feel safe as writers in order to take chances and develop a voice or even better themselves. If students don't think their work will be taken seriously or treated fairly, they won't take the chance to push themselves to try harder. This is particularly the case when it comes to sharing their writing with others and learning how to give peer feedback. Your students need to feel protected when they share their writing in that they will be treated fairly by their peers, which means that they must be taught how to give feedback in specific and constructive ways. That means that you, as the teacher, must find safe ways for students to share their writing and to keep track of student feedback so that you can be sure students are supporting one another while offering substantive response.

Blogs, wikis, and digital stories present safe ways for students to use new technologies to support their writing as part of the literacy classroom. As the teacher, you can control the level of publication or audience you wish your students to engage in—from a classroom blog to group blogs to individual blogs—and you can choose to password-protect blogs and comments. While students are reading and writing to the Web at large, you can control who sees the blog, even as students learn to write with a particular audience in mind. You might have students post samples of their writing to a classroom blog and choose to password-protect it so that only you and the students in the classroom can see the writing and the comments. This protection offers a level of safety to your students while still allowing them access to one another's writing and the opportunity for feedback, which you can view through the comments section. Or, students can use individual blogs to post their writing, which you and their peers can access via student-set passwords, again protecting the student while allowing access.

The same is true with wikis—you can set the amount and level of collaboration, although the responsibility of collaborating on something to be used by the classroom community is often enough to act as a safeguard and keep students not only honest but striving to do their best work, since it can be seen by their peers, teachers, parents, and community. A classroom wiki of student writing could be password-protected so that only those with access could read published writing.

Students also need to feel safe when sharing their thinking through writing, not just the writing itself. For example, you might decide to create a blog that teaches students to respond to reading through writing. One of your objectives, however, might be that you want students to learn how to engage in a debate about ideas while still being supportive and constructive with one another. You could do one of two things: you could either create an anonymous blog where students post using pseudonyms (you would keep a list with students' real names for your own reference) or you could create a password-only blog where students must have a password in order to access the blog and the post. Either way would protect the student, the first through anonymity and the second by allowing access only to members of the class. Also, as the teacher, you could monitor the posts and remove any that you don't feel are appropriate to the discussion (because you created the blog, you have the power to do this).

You may be asking, but why use a blog if I am going to limit access? Well, a blog is still public to the students within the classroom. You are still creating a public, shared space for students where they can learn to trust one another and participate in a written dialogue. As they become more comfortable with using this form of online conversation and critique, you might use your classroom blog for students to workshop pieces of writing, or debate ideas and content from class discussions, among other ideas. Because this is *their* space, too, and because the forum is open to others in the class, students tend to put in more time and energy and are much more respectful of one another. They like having an audience where their voice matters, as well as a safe space where they can try out new ideas.

The publication of digital stories, too, can be done in very safe ways. Not all digital stories need to end up on YouTube—they might do best on a classroom blog or wiki, or shared privately in class. With digital stories, movies aren't ready for publication until they are polished and you and the student storytellers decide to share them, thereby giving the locus of control to you and the authors of the story. Digital stories can easily be created in ways that do not share student names or identifying characteristics but still tell compelling stories and important historical information. These projects and tools are used throughout the literacy classroom, giving you oversight and helping you work with students in determining what is appropriate to share and when, an even higher standard than writing it for the teacher alone might previously have been. The safety resides in the steps you and your students take in creating and disseminating the story.

Authenticity

We know that students are much more motivated to engage in literacy tasks that are genuine than those that seem like busywork divorced from any real-world context. Learning is much more likely to transfer, too, when students read and write in the classroom in ways similar to how they do outside of schools. Many assessments and tools we use in schools are bound by school contexts and often seem useless to students, who may not understand why they are being asked to do what they are doing. It's essential to connect the kinds of reading and writing we ask our students to do for school purposes to the kinds of reading and writing that are important in the world so that they can learn to be literate in larger contexts than mere test taking or standardized assessments.

Blogs, wikis, and digital storytelling may seem much more legitimate to students than many other classroom tools because they are designed to support students and share projects with others. People other than the teacher are going to read, use, or view what the student has created or written, which can make the project seem more valuable and worthwhile. One of the main purposes for literacy is to communicate and connect with others. Yet this point is often lost in assignments that are simply turned in to the teacher or restricted to school use. As well, because wikis, blogs, and digital stories can make use of resources available online, they are easily connected to real-life issues and ideas that students find more interesting and important. Moreover, students can use texts and text types, such as online video and images, that may not be used in many literacy classrooms on a regular basis but that are part of their lives outside of school. Using blogs, wikis, and digital storytelling for learning purposes more closely mirrors the practices of students' lives and teaches valuable skills such as critiquing, understanding what to trust, and knowing what to use online outside of school.

If you think about any author today, chances are that he or she does not write in longhand on sheets of paper. This book, for example, was drafted using a software, called Scrivener, specifically designed for complex writing projects. It allowed me to draft chapters, put together note cards and outlines, and automatically generate a table of contents. Only then did I translate the manuscript into Microsoft Word in order to send it to my editor. Authentic reading and writing tasks today involve technological tools—whether word processors, online research, reading online texts, or more. Only in schools do we have large groups of people writing by hand for set amounts of time. In the workplace, most writing is done using technology, often by more than one person.

One good example of an authentic practice is a project resource wiki developed by a group of students. As we do research today, we must sift through enormous amounts of material, much like panning for gold. By creating a wiki, students can construct a place to put all those resources, which can be actively used and reused throughout the project. Students are constructing something they will actually use, that has meaning to them, and that potentially can be used by others.

The same thing holds true for digital storytelling. Students aren't learning the tools and skills involved with digital storytelling just to learn them. Rather, they are using their technological skills to create a narrative that is cohesive and contains the elements necessary to make that narrative successful. In both the wiki and the digital story, learning the technology goes hand in hand with learning the literacies of research and design in order to construct narratives and conduct project-based learning. With all of these tools, the literacy practices learned are learned for use, not just for themselves.

Practice

Literacy skills develop through practice. No one is born literate; we are all in the process of becoming and developing as readers and writers. As literacy teachers, we need to give our students ongoing opportunities to practice their reading and writing in engaging ways. Students take up practices using blogs, wikis, and digital stories easily and incorporate them across their lives in a variety of spaces, both educational and nonschool related. If we push them to think critically and increase their reading and writing activities using blogs, wikis, and digital narratives, these digital literacy practices will become natural and intrinsic, and take on importance in their lives. Our students will become increasingly comfortable with using digital tools to think out loud, to add to existing forms of online knowledge, to use visual means to tell important stories, and more.

Blogs are one good way to establish a writing practice through new literacies. If you use individual student blogs, they should be visited and added to often—similar in a sense to journal writing, but public and interconnected. I have found that having students write at least once a week, and pairing up students to respond to each other's posts, is key. A regular routine establishes blogging as a writing practice, and as students become comfortable with writing to make sense of their world, they start to become writers.

Relevance

One of the issues with teaching adolescents today is relevance. Sadly, the curriculum we love and work so hard over is frequently seen as completely disconnected from our students' thoughts and cares. Yet today, more than ever, literacy is central to everything they do. Blogs, wikis, and digital stories underscore this point. They are all about literacy. When students blog about what they read and create a classroom community through interconnected, personal blogs, we use the modern idea of social networking to teach the traditional technique of writing to respond to literature in a way our students understand, with a new technology they find motivating. Allowing students to craft narratives through digital storytelling still requires a written script with all the traditional characteristics of a story—setting, characters, plot, climax—but because the story is told visually, it can and will help support students who struggle with committing a written story to paper by allowing them to create a story in an alternative format with construction of a working script. Digital technologies bring literacy practices to where our students are without dumbing them down in any way—if anything, these tools can make practices more challenging.

With digital stories, for example, students can tell their own stories or persuade an audience—something that teens love to do and is a key skill for adolescents to learn. Because digital stories work best when researched, scripted or storyboarded, and well rehearsed, they meet many of the goals of a persuasive genre and can complement a piece of persuasive writing. Students can interview their peers and bring teen voices into the community through these stories.

Similarly, student blogs inject student voice into the classroom conversation. Because blogs are public, choosing them as a genre makes clear to your students that what they say (or write) matters. You can use student blogs as a part of a project, theme, or unit on memoir or throughout the year as ongoing writing practice. You might use blogging as a way for students to write about books they have read—to record their recommendations and thoughts. Or you might have students blog in response to current events, politics, or the world. Whatever the topic, narrow or broad, student blogging allows student thought to be an important part of the conversation and makes what your students think and feel relevant.

Meaning and Identity

We know that literacy practices are central to who we are, but we don't usually capitalize on this in the literacy classroom. We do some creative writing with our students, but we too easily forget that any writing involves putting oneself out there. Instead, we must teach and support community and self-development through writing, research, and collaboration. Blogs enable students to create a space for self—to decorate, name, and write the self into being while interacting with others through commenting. Wikis give groups a chance for collaboration and a space to build knowledge over time, to create meaning. And digital stories are a place to engage in that most basic of personal journeys: storytelling, whether from a creative or historical perspective, whether telling your own story or someone else's.

I have seen students create personal blogs that represent them through use of color, name, and photos (mostly pictures of themselves, often with their pets). I have gotten to know my students better because they have opened up a little. Seeing the Yankees logo on their blog, I know to ask about the score from the game last night, or about a new car mentioned in a post. I can know when a student is upset because the family pet had to be put to sleep or who has a big audition coming up. Because we know these things about each other, there's a level of connection and closeness that's missing when class is more anonymous, and with that level of connection comes students who are more willing to take a chance, to push themselves in their writing, to look for more meaning.

One of the things I enjoy most is using student blogs to respond to readings from class. Because blogs are written, I can see changes over time—a development—as students start to take more chances, respond to my questions in the comment field, ask themselves questions of their own. Some of the students begin to look deeper for meaning and even add links and connections to other information online, and I get to watch that understanding literally unfold.

With wikis and digital stories, the development of meaning comes through students working together to create a project that presents the results of research and writing, and that represents each student. Whether students are constructing a wiki of resources on stories of the Holocaust or a digital story about local history, part of the process of completing the project comes from negotiating a personal sense of themselves with a developing sense of the meaning of the work.

In all three cases, the digital tools provide opportunities for students to push themselves, develop a sense of who they are, and work toward deeper meaning.

Interest and Inquiry

Definitely one of the most important things we can do to motivate our students is to build on their interests and innate sense of inquiry. Many alternative schools, from home schools to charter schools to schools within a school, have been built around this idea. But it doesn't have to be that difficult or that intensive. Just making use of what's available online can be enough, especially if you use tools that allow you and your students to link up to the virtually infinite number of resources out there. We all have assessments and genres we have to teach, but often the content is open or at least flexible. Through blogs, wikis, and digital stories, students can search for, write about, and use online resources to research and create content based on ideas they find personally meaningful and interesting—giving them reason to want to be there, in your class, day after day—a definite change from simply mandating attendance. We want our students to be natural inquirers, to follow a genuine interest and create a desire to learn about something merely because they want to learn about it. Through contructing a blog or creating a wiki in response to a project, they can do just that—and these kinds of tools give them power and a voice. Digital stories, in particular, allow them to create content, something that is increasingly important in the world of Web 2.0.

For another example, students can choose a topic for a research project and, instead of turning in a traditional research paper with bibliography, can create a project wiki. Say the student chooses to research the life and work of

Edgar Allan Poe. That student (or students, if you choose to have them work in groups) can create a wiki instead of writing a research paper. Individual pages on the wiki can be devoted to different topics: Poe's life, his poetry, his short stories, why we continue to study Poe today. Each page might contain a written piece, not unlike a paper, but instead of a bibliography at the end of the overall project, each page would connect to resources on that topic. So if one page was about Poe's poetry, the page could contain a summary and analysis of his important work along with links to his poems, like this online page with the entire text of "The Raven": www.heise.de/ix/raven/Literature/Lore/TheRaven.html. Being able to directly link to the information enriches the project; allowing students to choose and research areas of interest builds on their own desire to inquire.

Because there is so much information online, we need to teach students how to research online effectively and how to write about what they find. You might try using a classroom blog to help students conduct research; in this blog, you could post instructions on the main page on how to conduct research. Students could then post the questions that they intend to use to frame their research; subsequent posts could outline where they are going to look for sources, links to what they have found, and so forth. Those posts, then, would become an informal way to assess how students are doing and to check on the sources they are using. You could do the same with student blogs—have students post about their research process as a way of keeping tabs on how it is going.

In my college class, students conducted a group research project, on a topic they chose, relating either to *Three Cups of Tea*, a book we read, or to current events in Pakistan and Afghanistan. First, I had the students post their research questions on their blogs so that I could comment on them and help them shape a question that was neither too broad or too narrow. Then, students posted about how they were conducting research—what search engines they were using as well as helpful links they found. I was able to go through these posts and check sources by clicking on the links. If a source wasn't valid or reliable, I could comment on the post or talk to the student in class about why. This kind of transparency allowed students to conduct their own inquiry projects in areas of interest while still being supported and learning how to do research online.

Perhaps the best example, though, of a digital technology that builds on student interest and inquiry is the digital story. Our students love to tell stories and are becoming increasingly comfortable documenting their lives in front of the camera. But they may never have thought about using digital video in an academic sense to present information. Digital stories, as mentioned before, are often most appealing to students who struggle in the literacy classroom because they provide another mode of expression—another way to show what they know.

I've already mentioned the digital history project from East Orange as one good example, but there are many others. Digital stories can be used to construct a response to literature, to present a persuasive argument in the form of a public service announcement, or to create and perform a piece of writing. Since a digital story contains both performance and publication in the form of a digitally preserved film, digital stories serve to legitimize your students' words and ideas—which in turn supports student interest and inquiry. And because almost any digital story project requires research, inquiry is built into every project.

Cognitive Development

Our students continue to develop over time, but how often do we record that growth? We can collect assessments over the course of the semester or the year, but the assessments are often disjointed, with different kinds of writing or tests that show many different pictures. A student's blog, however, displays a trajectory of cognitive development through writing that even the student can see and reflect on. How did I change? What did I think at the beginning of my blog compared to how I see things now? Or a project wiki—What were the questions we had when we began this project? What did we learn and how did we learn it? A digital story, too, can be the story of *how* we learn something as much as *what* we learn when a reflective piece is included. A short conclusion, added by the student or students on what was discovered through the project, offers important insight into the cognitive development of the student.

As I have used blogs with my students, I have come to see their individual development change just over the course of a semester. Even with the use of student blogs in response to reading, student posts change from short, surface-level comments to detailed analyses and questioning. With a classroom blog, I have observed how students foster discussion among one another, the kinds of questions they ask, and who participates and to what degree. Since all participation comes in the form of writing, we have a semipermanent record of student thinking and work that we can draw on, not just for grading, but for understanding how our students are faring in terms of cognitive development.

Take *The Secret Life of Bees* blog. Students created chapter guides and responses that their teacher could then use to determine how well the students were doing with comprehending and analyzing the material. She was also able to use the students' comments to the posts to see how well students responded to the study guides and understood the key themes of the book. In some ways, using a blog is like being able to extend discussion and keep a transcript at the same time—an invaluable source of information about how your students are doing in terms of comprehending and interacting with the text and the discussion.

With wikis, the proof is in both the writing and the links the student or students create. If you have students create a project wiki, you can assess the writing on different pages as well as the validity and usefulness of the links they include. A wiki created to help persuade people not to text while driving might have a main page that outlines the rest of the wiki; subsequent pages could detail different aspects of the argument along with links to news stories and research about the dangers of texting while driving. The wiki then would allow you to assess the students' ability to construct an argument in both a written and a hypertextual sense through the inclusion of links; you can assess how well students did their research as well as the kinds of sites and information they chose to include. The wiki overall then becomes a concrete representation of student thinking.

Community

Students generally come to our classes for one subject period, and then they're off again to their next class—a moment in time. They do their assignments at night and turn them in to us the next day. But as we know, with group projects, collaboration creates important connections between classmates that support learning and communication—we know better what we can explain to others. Classrooms that become communities support deeper student learning and encourage students to feel safer and take chances as writers and readers.

Wikis and blogs can extend what is learned in a classroom well beyond its physical walls and the hours of a single period. Students' blogging and commenting after class, or contributing to a blog, broadens the classroom community to include times and spaces past designated school hours and create relationships that will be reinforced in class and will help support learning.

In the prefreshman summer program, using blogging with the students allowed us to create a summer community that continued to make and sustain connections beyond the summer and into their first semester—an important support network for what can be the toughest semester for college students. Their development as readers and writers continued after class ended, and as the program progressed their blog posts and comments grew in length and developed in sophistication. They offered each other better, deeper commentaries on their presentations and research. Without this tool, the class would have ended each day devoid of these additional connections, and the essential sense of community they developed would have been lost.

Many of the blogs mentioned in previous chapters knit together the members of a class into a community. The best and perhaps simplest way to do this may be through a classroom blog. You can create a classroom blog easily and as soon as you start using it to showcase student work, report on new projects, and keep parents in the loop, you have moved toward creating a community that extends beyond the classroom and the school day. You might choose to create a classroom blog around a particular unit—say, poetry—in order to publish student poems, put up links to poems of the day (April is National Poetry Month; a class blog could be used to showcase a link to a different poem each day for parents and students to read together, and even respond to), and connect the unit to other activities on the Web more generally—poetry sites, famous authors' pages, and more.

The same can be done with wikis. Project or classroom wikis around specific topics or classes can be used for students to connect to one another through reading each other's work, responding to posts, putting up links of interest related to the topic, and so on. Because wikis and blogs make space for student voice, they open up that space to a community where students feel valued and get to know one another in a deeper sense than just as classmates. Students are also taking on the responsibility for posting and keeping the blogs and wikis; that responsibility, too, goes a long way toward building a community.

> Wikis and blogs allow space for student voice, and they also carry with them responsibility for posting comments and text. In this way they contribute to building and opening up a safe community where students can feel valued and begin to know one another in a deeper sense.

And last but not least, creating digital stories together puts students in the position of learning from one another, stitching together into one voice a question or topic that means something to them. I have seen students put extensive time and energy into digital stories—and get out of it deeper relationships to one another. The fifth and eighth graders in East Orange would never have worked together under any other circumstance, nor would my college reading students have told their stories of hardship as recent immigrants or as the first in their families to attend college without that sense of community and trust.

Process

We know that writing and reading are part of a process of literacy development over time. We plan, write, edit, and rewrite when we write in the real world, and many of us use the process approach to teach writing in our classrooms. We also know that reading is an active process that involves interacting with texts, discussing and responding to them, and recommending or critiquing books and readings. Digital tools are excellent ways to support the reading and writing process in your classroom. Blogs and wikis can be used not only to post in response to reading or collect resources for projects, but also to post drafts of writing and get comments and feedback from peers. Many of us struggle with how to teach students the process approach to writing in ways that help them with the drafting and peer editing aspects of the process, and here are free, online tools that allow students to post writing where a peer can access it from any computer with an Internet connection and, additionally, use the commenting feature to peer edit. Multiple people can read it, and a classroom blog (as some of the examples in this chapter showed) can be used to publish class writing and feature finished pieces. It's an excellent, easy publication tool, as is a wiki, since countless pages with published writing can be added readily. Student blogs can also be used as brainstorming spaces for new writing ideas or places to gather research links that you can check in on to see where your students are in the writing process without having to collect papers in various forms. Instead, just put up a page on a class blog or wiki with links to each student's blog and have access to all of them—there, in one place.

This could be a two-part process. First, you might set up a classroom blog where everyone could participate and post pieces of writing. Other students would comment and, through the commenting process, learn how to give constructive feedback. Because comments would be seen by others as well as you, students would be pressured to write something more substantive and less generic; also, since their names are attached to the comments (if you choose), they don't have the protection of anonymity to be cruel. Comments on writing are much more likely to be helpful and useful rather than malicious or useless, particularly if the class has become a community through the use of new technologies like these.

Say you have students working on the genre of memoir. They could workshop first lines and first paragraphs by posting them on the class blog and inviting feedback. Having a public forum often pushes students to do better work, as well as learn from others about what makes for good writing, a good lead, and good feedback. You could also post in your own responses examples of good memoir opening lines or links to classic memoirs, for instance.

As students move into completing pieces, the class could construct a memoir wiki that would publish student work on separate pages. The main or opening page could have a description of the assignment and genre, along with links to each student's page and piece. On each page, a student would publish his or her piece, along with any visuals—photos, or even links that extend or make sense within the written work.

Outstanding pieces might end up as excellent digital stories. The memoir itself would be an excellent script, read aloud and set to images and music. The writing is still there and, in fact, serves as the backbone or structure of the piece. Extending it into a digital story just allows for the visual aspects of a memoir to flow, matching word to image.

So the writing process can be applied across all three tools, moving from early stages of work posted on a blog through polished pieces published on a wiki or transmediated or transformed through the addition of visual and musical elements into a digital story. The underlying idea remains the same: writing and rewriting to create and carefully construct a polished piece of work—not as an individual but through a process involving a community.

Motivation

What it all comes down to is motivation. What motivates our students? We see the best work, the most interest, and the highest engagement when students are motivated to learn and participate. For some of our students, the literacy classroom is fraught with difficulty. They struggle with reading and writing and we work hard to reach them. We have to find ways and tools that motivate our least motivated students, to bring them into the class conversation and engage them in learning. When we use new technologies, when we connect what we teach to their lives, when we give them the opportunity to research, write, and create from topics of interest to them, when we establish a classroom community, and when we understand that literacy is intricately intertwined with who they are and how they see the world, we create paths of motivation for them to engage with literacy learning in our classrooms. The students we are teaching today, whether you call them digital natives, twenty-first-century learners, or just teenagers, are motivated by new technologies, ideas that engage them, the possibilities of being able to create something that is their own, and the concept of being heard for who they are. Using new technologies like blogs, wikis, and digital stories is one way to do that—as I and countless other teachers, from New Jersey to Australia and Singapore to Colorado have learned. I hope you do, too.

Upcoming Technologies
That May Make a Difference
in the English Classroom

It's important to be aware of newer technologies as they appear, for two reasons: first, because they may be of use in your classroom, and second, because they may become an important part of students' lives that we can build on to motivate and engage students in literacy learning. Sometimes the connections between new technologies and literacies are clear. Other times we have to look deeply to see how students can use reading, writing, speaking, and listening to engage with new tools. This chapter outlines some new technologies not only because they may be of use to you in your classrooms, but also to keep you aware of new terms and new tools. These are just a few of the latest technologies on the horizon. Newer ones are right behind them, and by the time this is in print, chances are something even newer has made its debut. Keeping up to date on what appears on the technological front is vital in bridging the worlds of your literacy classroom and your students' outside lives.

One of the things about new technologies is that they seem to appear faster than we can assimilate them into our lives, yet our students can pick up and make use of them quickly. New shifts in terms and ideas underlie the latest developments, and these ideas are important in understanding how the changes impact learning and literacy. Many of us didn't really know the term *Web 1.0* before *Web 2.0* became the new buzzword. Or, we were just getting used to the idea of blogging and seeing blogs appear in the most unlikely places, such as the front page of the online version of the *New York Times*, when Twitter was unleashed on the world and all sorts of people were tweeting everything, from their dinner plans to political events. With all these new technologies come new questions: What is useful for education? Can these technologies be used with students and should they? What would happen if we used these new digital tools in classrooms?

There's a natural urge to jump on the bandwagon and try the newest technologies with students even when it may not be the best idea. That's not to say that new technologies aren't good for students. In fact, many districts and school administrations react in the exact opposite manner and ban new technologies without trying them in the classroom. In many cases, new technologies like Twitter are automatically either glorified or vilified. Throughout this book, I have tried to make the point that technologies are tools, nothing more—in and of themselves, they are neither good nor bad. The question is not whether or not to use technology overall, but which tools to choose based on what you want to do with them.

The right technology is the tool that allows you to do what you need to do with it—the blog that gets the less motivated student to start writing because he knows other people will care about what he has to say now that he has a voice, for example. Or the digital story project that will help teach students how to persuade their audience using the traditional components of persuasive writing along with new media.

Some of the newest technologies profiled here may not be used much yet in school environments but are making waves in popular media and our students' lives. The intention is to give you a sense of what these tools are and how they work so you can understand what something like Twitter is, join in the conversation, and make an informed decision. The two questions to ask yourself are these:

1. Is this a tool that will fit the purpose I have in my classroom?
2. How can I use this technology to fit a specific purpose in my classroom (rather than using it simply because it is new)?

Asking yourself these questions will help keep you from rushing into using a technology simply because it is the hot new thing. As you read this chapter, keep in mind what your purposes and goals are in terms of your literacy instruction and your students' literacy practices. You may come away with a deeper knowledge of the digital tools that are indispensable to our students in nonacademic ways—an important aspect of understanding the new literacies of our students. Some of these technologies, like Twitter, are so new that we really don't know too much yet about how they can be used educationally— but of course that doesn't mean they can't be.

Once you have read through the descriptions of these latest technologies, I recommend you spend some time with them online—create an account and try using them yourself to get a sense of how they work. Even if you never use a tool like Twitter in your teaching, you will get a better sense of how it works and why it has become so popular in such a short time, as well as how language and literacy work within this new technology.

Some of the technologies I will discuss in this chapter are controversial because they are popular with teenagers and are considered to be everything from dangerous and nonacademic to violent and confusing to adults. These technologies make up much of the social worlds of our students and may not have a clear place in the classroom, and yet some teachers have found success in using them as a jumping-off place to get kids engaged in the literacy curriculum.

Whether you use these tools or just read this chapter to be more informed, these are technologies that our students rely on, are learning more about, and are developing increased expertise in—every day. This chapter will discuss literacy practices on social networking sites like MySpace and Facebook (and the educational uses of sites that build on the ideas of social networking, such as Ning), micro-blogging through sites like Twitter, social bookmarking using sites like Delicious (formerly del.icio.us), gaming and literacy practices, and literacy through mobile tools and devices like texting and cell phones.

Literacy Practices and Social Networking

As mentioned in Chapter 1, many teens spend an enormous amount of time online connecting through social networks like MySpace and Facebook. For both of those sites (Facebook being the larger with more than 300 million members as of October 2009), literacy and language are the currency of the realm. Even with the use of pictures and video, members primarily use language to represent themselves through status reports, self-descriptions, quotes, responses to friends' comments, and so forth. What's important to remember is that these comments and words don't really go away—all these posts and statements are stored somewhere. Language use on the Web has permanence—as anyone who has dealt with a student upset over an online posting knows. These are written interchanges, and as such are as much like letters as conversations, despite their use of slang and casual phrasing and style.

Our students use language and literacy to create a sense of identity across these sites that is at the very least semipermanent and that can leave a trail that will follow them for some time. These trails are accessible not just to friends but to family, employers, teachers, administrators, and other members of the community—something many of our students may never stop to consider. Because social networking is seen as an interchange between friends, the semipermanent and searchable nature of these exchanges is often forgotten and students can be caught up short when it comes time to apply for jobs, colleges, and scholarships, for instance. For a generation that has never written traditional letters, the idea that these kinds of interactions can indeed be saved and printed out may be a foreign one. Literacy practices are just that, literate interchanges—and as such, they have a permanence that historically has been saved as letters and diaries. Social networks, in a sense, are the diaries and letters of this generation and, since networks like Facebook save the content of their sites to their servers, none of these interactions is ever lost. It's an essential point, and one rarely ever raised. Perhaps we, as teachers, have to be the ones to do so. Literacy is important because it allows us to shape who we are through the language we use—but it also leaves a trace, a trail that others can use to remember who we are. Our words tell others who we are, so we must be careful how we use them.

The idea of a social networking site as an identity marker has been used successfully by some teachers through projects like having students create a MySpace site for a famous person—an author or historical figure, for instance. What would Abraham Lincoln include on his MySpace site? How would he define himself? Or J. K. Rowling? What kinds of information would such a person choose to include and make public? Discussing these issues with students makes concrete the idea that some information should be public and perhaps some should not. Because anyone who chooses to can access this person's profile, certain decisions need to be made. A student may not have thought those decisions through quite so carefully with his or her own profile. By creating or discussing the creation of a profile for someone else (what should President Obama put on his MySpace page?), these decisions become more concrete. Actually, the President did use Facebook when he was running for office and has used Facebook since his election, but his page is very particular in the information it does and does not include—which can lead to an excellent discussion about issues of audience when writing as well as divisions between the public and private nature of information online.

When it comes to literacy practices and social networking, it is quite possible that MySpace and Facebook for the most part do not really belong in the literacy classroom. Yet, because they occupy such a central role in the lives of our students, they often end up there—whether from an issue raised because of something someone posted about another student, through a problem with cyberbullying, or because of parental concerns raised in your district. As literacy practices become increasingly embedded with technological practices, we have to teach our students about the nature of information, privacy, and protection as well as writing and identity. However or whether you choose to address these issues with your students, social networking is probably a central part of their lives. It is important for them to understand that how they shape this writing is key to how others see them. Writing is still an essential way to make their identity known, and they have the power to control that information.

The idea of social networking is now making its way into education through the development of social networking sites devoted to educational communities. The best-known and most frequented example of this is Ning (www.ning.com/), a free, online social networking site that allows teachers or anyone else to create a site for users to post blogs, interact through a discussion, put up personal pages, and more. Because the idea behind social networks online is to connect people, online social networking for classes and students makes perfect sense—especially when you can use a free site like Ning without having to go through a site like Facebook or MySpace that may contain controversial information or be blocked by your district. Since you set up the Ning, or social network, you maintain control—you choose who to invite to be a part of the network, who can see it (i.e., whether it is fully public or private and restricted to users only), and which components you want to use.

Ning includes features such as built-in blogs for each user or the class, a discussion forum, a chat area, a notes section that includes the capability to link to Web pages and video, and a space to post events. Some teachers have moved to using Ning rather than more traditional courseware systems like Blackboard since it is free, easy to use, can be made public so that others besides class members can see it (if you want parents, other teachers, community members, or other classes to participate, for example), and can be viewed from any computer with an Internet connection regardless of the operating system. It's easy to set up and maintain, which makes it an excellent choice if you want to incorporate social networking tools into your classroom.

So even though MySpace and Facebook are not be the kinds of technologies you think of when you think about incorporating digital tools into your teaching, the concept of social networking for working with your students beyond the classroom may be a valuable one for you. A free site like Ning might be a great tool to try, especially since you, as the teacher, maintain control over its use, access, and content. One of the great strengths of Web 2.0 tools is the connections they allow us to make to others, and social networking is one good example.

Micro-blogging and Twitter

Twitter is the newest technology to hit the public imagination, perhaps because of its ease of use or because it's a constant source of information, relevant or not. While blogging in the sense that has been used throughout this book involves setting up and maintaining a personal or group website, "tweeting" is like text messaging to the world at large, 140 characters at a time. A user signs up on the site Twitter.com (http://twitter.com/), and anyone who locates that user can choose to follow him or her and read the "tweets," as they are known, as soon as they are posted.

Twitter was created in 2006 by Jack Dorsey (according to Wikipedia and the About page on the Twitter site), the former CEO of Twitter. It was built on the same model as text messaging but with the idea of posting to a group or world at large, and the initial motivation was to be able to post information when going out to bars and clubs about what was happening and where. From there, tweeting became a way to inform the world (or at least anyone who is following you) about everything from what was for breakfast to where to meet for protests against the election in the streets of Tehran.

While tweets are often about quotidian experiences, celebrities, politicians, and even officials from the White House representing President Obama are tweeting—part of an overall attempt to keep the world "in the loop." Although this may epitomize a world that believes that everything must be public knowledge, and that any or even the smallest bit of information is worthy of making public, everyone from Oprah to state representatives are using Twitter to keep the world informed from second to second. Newscasters and television shows make references to tweets, and office workers slyly tweet during meetings. It would seem that we are moving ever further into an age of too much information that feeds into our addiction to know as much as we can, as soon as we can. Yet, as we saw during the recent election in Iran, when you cross micro-blogging with social networking by allowing people to instantly message anyone in their social group, these tools can organize groups in much more meaningful ways than traditional methods can. The use of Twitter became so widespread at one point that the Iranian government tried to shut down the site, but because it is a service and not localized in one site, protestors were able to continue to send tweets to organize protests and get information out (Cohen 2009).

In order to see the tweets of the people you follow, whether your best friends or your favorite movie star, you can either keep Twitter.com open or download a sidebar application like Twitterific, TwitterFox, or Seesmic that lets you surreptitiously check for new tweets through your Web browser or in a separate application in a more low-key way (there's even an application that loads tweets into what looks like an Excel spreadsheet so that it really looks like you're working hard). But what are the possible educational applications of a technology like this?

Truth be told, there may not be many. Certainly, much of what gets posted to Twitter is the electronic equivalent of navel gazing. But there are two ways that Twitter has been very useful to me. First, tech-savvy teachers who use technology well in their classrooms, as well as those interested in learning more about new technologies, tend to have accounts on Twitter—such as Mark Wagner, Clay Burell, and Will Richardson, and the like. Their tweets, rather than being merely detailed posts about what they are doing right that second, often have links to good online educational technologies and new ideas for the classroom. And because Twitter delivers messages to you rather than the other way around, you don't have to go to and read their blogs each day. Following technology-interested educators on Twitter can enrich your own practice and, of course, you can ignore anything that isn't useful to you. Through their tweets, I have had access to excellent sites and information online that I never would have found otherwise.

The other way Twitter might be helpful to you and your students is through following politicians, news journalists, educators, and others whose tweets reflect the intricacies of life in those professions. I follow the *New York Times* technology reporter David Pogue online through Twitter to keep up-to-date about new technology developments. Other services have a Twitter feed you can follow. The White House has chosen to join Twitter under the username BarackObama; by following BarackObama, you and your students can get real-time updates of information from the White House on current issues. This surpasses reading the newspaper, even online. In fact, an interesting comparison might be made between the news available in a paper newspaper, the online version, and a micro-blogging site like Twitter, which is able to update information immediately.

There are two ways to search for information on Twitter: by looking for a person to follow or by using the search engine to look for a topic. But searcher beware. Like any wide-open network, Twitter will allow whatever tweeters think about a topic. For this reason, Twitter might be blocked in your district (although you may be able to make a pretty compelling case for unblocking the site in order to follow the White House, for example). If you're looking for the fastest source of information on a breaking story like the swine flu, Twitter might be the best place to find it—and it's a great place to teach students how to determine the accuracy of a source. A tweet from the White House or a Senator's office or a *New York Times* reporter like David Pogue can be seen very differently than a tweet from someone whose credentials are quite different or who has no clear credentials at all.

Twitter might not be your cup of tea, and it might not serve a clear purpose for your classroom right now, but as more and more technologies move toward serving the growing needs of delivering information immediately, whether verified or not, these applications will only continue to grow. As with social networking, the question may not be, how can I use this in my classroom, but how do I understand this technology and the impact it may have on the language and literacy practices of my students and my world? Since Twitter limits its messages to 140 characters, the emphasis is on the short and sweet. There are publishers who are working to release stories told in Twitter serials, which raises the questions, How do we engage students in understanding and enjoying longer, connected text when new technologies like Twitter move us toward shorter and shorter messages? How do we teach them a variety of strategies and appreciation for all of these kinds of writing? The answer may come as our own familiarity and comfort with these new kinds of technologies and tools grows.

Literacy and Gaming

One of the most controversial technologies impacting the lives of students today are video games. Many researchers and hundreds of studies (see Funk et al. 2004 and Vandewater, Shim, and Caplovitz 2004, for examples) have examined issues like the relationship between video games and violence or video games and obesity. But an interesting and perhaps underexamined influence video games may have for our students is on their literacy practices. In his seminal work on video games, literacy, and learning, James Gee (2007) found that teens not only spend a lot of time gaming, but that the learning they engage in can represent sophisticated problem solving and can involve literacy as well.

It is undoubtedly true that many games are violent and that some lead to sedentary activity. But it is also true that the advent of gaming systems like the

Nintendo Wii incorporate movement and that gaming can allow for collaborative learning—for example, some games like Call of Duty have kids (and adults) talking together as well as playing together online—far from the preconception that teen gamers are loners playing on a basement couch for hours at a time. Teens and video games represent a more complex learning and literacy interaction than was first conceptualized, as Gee found out when he took it upon himself to learn a game in order to play with his son. Not only did he have to learn sophisticated problem-solving skills so as to move up levels and finally solve the game, but he found out that gamers spend time interacting with one another and reading and writing about games online and in gaming magazines in order to be successful. As well, some gamers create written works of fiction based on characters in the games—the fan fiction I talked about earlier. These stories are posted online and are often peer edited and commented on by other members of the fan fiction site.

Many video games are built around a narrative structure, with a specific setting, a character or characters that engage on a journey or a quest, a problem or problems, and an eventual climax. Yes, there's often violence, and that violence can be problematic, but it can also be an excellent source of discussion for students: Why is the level of violence in games like Call of Duty or Grand Theft Auto IV necessary? What does it do? Nevertheless, within the game, students are involved in complex learning activities and, often, literacy activities, in order to solve the game.

Many games have cheat and tips sites, magazines, and manuals that students pore over in order to figure out difficult levels or problems they encounter in the games. Some have complicated card and other games associated with them in which students play and memorize complex sets of rules, characters, and situations. Gaming is far from a "brain dead" occupation; many games require multiple levels of problem-solving and literacy practices in order to solve them, and gamers belong to different online and face-to-face communities around these games, several of which use literacy in order to interact and share information. Game spaces may be filled with language, and sites devoted to learning about the games and different cheats and tips contain online communities, chat rooms, and countless pages of information.

This is not to advocate for using games in the literacy classroom necessarily, but to raise awareness that gamers do engage in literacy activities, some of which may be valuable. Students may bring texts into class, such as gaming magazines, which may be appropriate to read during independent reading and may be very sophisticated expository text. Literature around gaming, including graphic novels (as long as you have either previewed them or gotten parent permission) can be a great way to get a student interested—first in reading, and then, in more "traditional" graphic novels (longer, more complex illustrated books than comic books) like *American-Born Chinese* or *Persepolis*.

Gaming is a big part of the literacy activities our students engage in outside of the classroom on a regular basis, so it makes sense to make room for those texts that are appropriate in classroom practices. In some ways, the narratives of certain games, particularly role-playing games, are similar to creative, digital stories; students can build on concepts of setting, character, interaction, problem, and more from their gaming practices.

Aside from gaming, other new practices have arisen around multimedia, immersive virtual worlds for kids, from Club Penguin and Webkinz (for young preteens) to Teen Second Life (for teens from thirteen to seventeen). Teen Second Life (http://teensecondlife.com) is an immersive, three-dimensional online world that only teenagers can join and where users choose and create an avatar, or representation of themselves. Through the Teen Second Life world, students can interact with peers from all over the world, create an online business, participate in learning activities, and learn to build in an online, three-dimensional environment. It's not a game per se; Teen Second Life was designed as a space to encompass interactions, building, learning, and much more. It is operated for free by Linden Labs in San Francisco, and only authorized adults vetted by the company can be a part of the environment. (For an example of an adult Second Life you can participate in, go to www.secondlife.com.) Interactions with others in Second Life, whether Teen or adult, are mostly done through typing and can be done in the language of the member.

The point here is this: our students are increasingly used to interacting with others online, whether through social networking or, now, collaborative gaming and online environments. Many of these interactions are text based and done through linguistic means—and they are very important to many of our students. You obviously can steer clear of gaming in the classroom, but using texts about games and gaming or building on structures of game elements in your teaching can help you reach out to those students traditionally alienated in the literacy classroom.

Literacy Through Mobile Tools

Ah, yes. If you teach teenagers, you know about texting via cell phone. Chances are, you've seen it in your classroom, you may text yourself, and you may have graded at least one paper where an abbreviation or two meant for a text chat made an appearance. Texting is the black sheep of the technology world when it comes to literacy. Purists of the English language (and probably other languages too, although I can't write with expertise about that) worry that texting is corrupting the ways in which we use English and, at least at first, that seemed to be the case. But the thing is, we use language in a particular way for a particular audience any time we use it. If you use an abbreviation like *cu l8r* in the wrong place, it's a bad choice based on audience, not a bastardization of the English language per se. *See you later* still exists, it was just replaced by something else when it shouldn't have been.

As literacy teachers, we've always had the responsibility of teaching our students to pay attention to language use, audience, and purpose. As in, "You're writing this to turn it in, so use proper English" is just another way of saying "Pay attention to the audience, purpose, and language use because it all counts." Whether you are writing a card to your mother for Mother's Day or a text to your best friend, the situation, audience, and purpose all determine how you use language. The development of new forms doesn't have to replace the older forms.

This is not to say that texting is a form of writing that has its place in the literacy classroom, unless it is an example of teaching about audience, form, and purpose. Yet it is a text type now, used millions of times a minute, all over the world. Our students are as or more likely to text than make a phone call, and they send hundreds of texts a week. This is a form of communication that has taken precedence in their lives, and they have come to rely on it, so much so that students often fall back into the language of texting as a matter of course. The best way to combat this is to bring to the foreground the issue of audience and purpose whenever students are writing, as well as to value texting as another form of writing with a clear purpose and audience. When we denigrate texting and electronic forms of communication that are central to our students' lives, we lose standing in students' eyes for not understanding that which is important to them. On the other hand, if we approach all ways of writing and making meaning as appropriate in particular situations, we can get our students to start thinking more deeply about questions of form, purpose, audience, and text—the very issues that are key to us as writing and literacy teachers.

Interestingly, some writers are playing with the form, including Lauren Myracle, the author of the young adult book *ttyl*, which is written as a series of instant messages between three best friends in high school. The book, which is one of a series, is written entirely using abbreviations; the books are very popular among adolescents although they have not been as well received by adults and have even been banned in some areas, but more for their explicit material than their format. Their popularity speaks to the centrality of text messaging (or instant messaging via computer) in teens' lives, and how this form of writing not only makes sense for short, succinct messages but can actually even carry a narrative along. As literacy teachers, we must understand how different forms of language work in our students' lives. We must build on what our students already know and do well to teach them the languages they will need to be successful in the world.

Where Does That Leave Us?

While many of the technologies in this chapter aren't necessarily ones you might bring into your teaching directly, they all have implications for language and literacy in the lives of your students. Some, like Ning, have educational counterparts that are being used now in classrooms everywhere; some, like Twitter, are so new that their educational purposes are still being determined. Still others, like gaming and 3-D virtual environments, may seem too "out there"—beyond the purview of literacy teaching—to even think about. That's all right. The important "takeaway" from this chapter is simply this: new tools change the ways we use language and literacy in significant ways, and these are the newest tools. How they are changing language and literacy is still being decided, but after reading this, you can at least lay claim to knowing what a tweet is or how to address texting abbreviations that crop up in school assignments. Remember, we're all figuring this out as we go along—and what works for you is what works for you. No new technology should be used just because it is new. Choose that which is right for you and your students' literacy learning and teaching, and you're on the right path.

Conclusion

As school starts for another fall and, once again, I see students all around me, on their cell phones, draped over laptops, and listening to iPods, I think about how far digital technologies have come in such a short time. We can do things and communicate in ways that we only dreamt about just a few short years ago. We can send instant messages. We can publish what we write so anyone in the world can read it. We can create and post video to share with others. We can find out about virtually anything online.

Our students' lives are different than ours were as a result. These new technologies mean that teens can access much more information, stay much more connected, and participate in much more than we ever could at their age. They play games and network online in ways we are only beginning to understand. But at the bottom of it all, they're still teens and, what's most interesting, they're still reading, writing, and using language.

There's a lot of media attention around the idea that kids no longer read or write like they used to and that traditional literacy practices have fallen out of favor. Yet we live in a world where Harry Potter and Twilight have bred legions of fans devoted to every twist and turn of their sagas. This is an age where teens write fan fiction for intrinsic reasons. They read manga and graphic novels as well as young adult fiction. And they write and read using digital tools almost constantly. This ever-connected generation is always on, always reading and writing, typing, texting, posting, filming, uploading images—just to name a few of their practices. Millennials still use reading and writing to make sense of their world, just differently.

There is no shortage of texts and ways students make meaning using language and digital tools. These new literacies are as essential to their lives as we believe traditional literacies should be. Teaching reading and writing today means taking into account changes in how we make sense of our world through literacy as new tools grow in importance, but it doesn't mean focusing less on reading and writing themselves. In fact, reading and writing are more essential—not less.

We are, first of all, teachers and lovers of language, reading, and writing. While much of this book has been about technology, the thrust of it is really about how we read and write today. Choosing to use a new digital technology like a blog, wiki, or digital story in your classroom doesn't mean we are abandoning teaching students how to read or write effectively; it isn't a move away from traditional notions of what it means to read and write. We still decode, comprehend, and analyze when we read online. Instead, choosing to use a new technology means choosing to add a new tool to your arsenal, to help support student learning, engage and motivate reluctant readers and writers, extend cognitive development, and create communities of learners.

We live in a world where rapid change is the name of the game, but we're still the ones who make the decisions when it comes to effective literacy instruction in our classroom. In incorporating new tools, we help students learn how to read and write effectively for a new age that is expecting them to know how to think flexibly and use new literacies. Already we know that when we ask our students to do research, they go online rather than to the library, despite any recommendations to the contrary. We know that many, if not most, of our students spend hours on Facebook and other social networking sites, and that they see these practices as essential to their lives.

What we can do is build a bridge between what our students are doing online and in their lives and the ways in which they need to learn to read and write to be successful today. We can use blogs and wikis and digital stories to support them in their development as writers, readers, researchers, and thinkers because these tools will motivate our students and build on the technological expertise many of them already have.

I have seen students like Vinnie blossom from being sullen and disconnected to being open and curious once they felt engaged, motivated, and interested—and the change I made was to try using new tools that opened up the conversation to include them in new ways. Perhaps the best example came from the Witnessing History project in East Orange, New Jersey.

East Orange, New Jersey, is a very small town not far from Newark, sandwiched between the housing projects of Newark and the multimillion dollar homes of more affluent suburbs. We worked with both private and public middle schools on a small grant project that was just enough to provide each teacher with one digital video camera, one digital still camera, and one digital voice recorder. Each teacher had one computer in his or her classroom. One of the schools we worked with was a parochial school in one of the poorer parts of town; the school, primarily African American and Hispanic, was small and drew from the neighborhood, so these were truly East Orange kids. My colleague and I came from the university in order to support the teachers in using digital storytelling as a technique in their classroom. Not one of the teachers had done any kind of project like this before; in fact, most of the teachers we worked with had very limited technology available to them. The story I want to tell here is about two classrooms in that parochial school, in fifth and eighth grades, that worked together to produce a story about the history of East Orange from the Depression through the Civil Rights Movement.

Two of the teachers, one from fifth grade and one from eighth grade, decided to have their students work together on producing a single video. So that each student had a part, mixed groups of fifth- and eighth-grade students were set up and assigned tasks: writing research questions about the Depression, World War II, and the Civil Rights Movement; doing research online to answer these questions; writing interview questions and conducting interviews with community members; filming and taking pictures in the community; writing and recording voice-over text with information from the research group; using software to edit the video together.

My colleague and I visited the school on one of the project work days to observe. What I saw astounded me. About forty fifth and eighth graders, all in one room, were working hard on the project in their groups. Not a single student was off task or messing around—in fact, their focus and interest were almost eerie. As I traveled around the room asking questions of each group, students fired questions right back: Did I know that even restrooms were segregated during the Civil Rights Movement? What did I think about the fact that we now had a black president, given how bad things used to be for African Americans? Did I know that we were in a recession now that was being compared to the Great Depression?

With no prodding from the teacher, each group outlined for me what they were doing and why—how their piece would fit into the digital story as a whole. The voice-over group had divided the text they had written into pieces and were recording it, very seriously, without the giggles you might expect from middle school students. Another group told me of their experience interviewing the school secretary, who remembered the day World War II ended and going to Times Square to celebrate. Every student in that classroom that day was engaged in the project and every single one, when I asked, not only said that they preferred to learn history and English this way but that it was more "real" than reading about history in a book and writing a report.

The finished digital story, which ran a little over twenty minutes, was of professional quality. The teachers admitted they had had nothing to do with the technical aspects—the students had figured out all of the editing and scripting using the technology—and both teachers felt that the project had been an unqualified success, despite some misgivings they had had at first about putting fifth and eighth graders together to work. Both teachers were amazed at the level of engagement and the quality of work from all of their students—and by the fact that students taught themselves how to use the technology and how to collaboratively problem-solve putting the different pieces of the project together.

Even though this classroom wasn't filled with technology, even though these students may not have had the most recent new digital tools available to each of them, this project was successful. Each student learned more about both researching history and constructing an informational piece about their community because they were engaged and motivated. The fifth graders were learning at and above their level because they had the opportunity to work with the eighth graders, who then served as peer leaders and support for the younger students. Even though students were broken into groups to do the project, the results of the research and the formulating of the questions were shared among the classes so that everyone was on the same page in making the project. And the students themselves preferred it not just because the tools were new but because they themselves felt like they learned more, differently.

That's what including new literacies into the literacy classroom can do. We can build on student interest and expertise to make them a bigger part of what we do when we teach and learn reading and writing. We can give students a voice through blogging, we can allow them choice and give them the opportunity to construct their own learning through creating project wikis and digital stories. We can broaden what we mean by reading and writing to include new forms of literacy and new tools that will help us keep them motivated and help them learn more deeply. We can use these tools to measure learning over time, to connect to parents and other members of the community, to support students through the writing process.

We're still literacy teachers and, although literacy is changing, reading and writing are central to what we do. We can make space and create possibility when we open our teaching to new digital tools and practices, one step at a time. Just by trying one new tool we send the message that new literacies—new technologies and the ways we read and write using them—are important too. Our students live in this new technological age, and what is relevant to their lives is mediated by these new tools.

It's a stepwise progression. In no way should books or papers be left out of literacy instruction. The key is inclusion rather than substitution. If a new technology can serve you better in teaching and supporting your students' literacy development, then it's the right tool to use. Blogs, wikis, and digital stories are great places to start; they're free or cheap to use, they build on technology practices students already engage in, and they use reading and writing in ways that are familiar to the literacy classroom. With time, you may branch out into using newer tools—Twitter, gaming, virtual worlds. Who knows? The point is to see how a new technology works to shift learning and literacy in ways beneficial to you and your students. I've seen it happen as a teacher to my students, as an observer in many classrooms like the one in East Orange. I believe it can happen to you.

So welcome to the world of new literacies. You'll be amazed at what you and your students will discover.

Appendix
Helpful Online Resources

Blogs

http://areallydifferentplace.org/ is the Broken Arrow Enhanced Learning Center blog. This center is part of the mission school district in Shawnee, Kansas. Their classroom blog is a forum for both students and teachers to discuss books, writing assignments, movies, and plays. Each student can start their own personal blog in addition to contributing to the whole class discussions. Personal blog listings can be found on the left-hand column of the home page.

www.blogger.com is a free blog-publishing tool with a range of options for creating multiple author blogs. It includes a host of privacy settings, and the ability to moderate comments. Blogger is a great tool for creating a blog in which all members of your class can upload and contribute text and media. All of these attributes make this blogging platform ideal for a private or public classroom format. A small drawback is that although there are several options for personalizing the look of the blogs, there are very few options for changing the basic layout. However, the options for widgets and applications that can be added to Blogger-host blogs is unlimited, because the platform allows applications and widgets to be added from alternate sites.

http://bookwrap.edublogs.org is a blog set up by a year 3 classroom in Sydney, Australia. The main purpose of this class blog is to create discussion around books that the students are currently reading. The blog serves as a reading community for the students, where the goals are learning more about certain authors, discussing key parts of books, and testing out their voices as readers with important opinions and ideas.

http://dmcordell.blogspot.com is a blog by the educator Diane Cordell titled Journeys: Exploring Life and Learning. It is a blog worth looking at not only for its artistic and intellectual merits, but for its very soothing and reflective nature. The site is filled with exquisite photography, paintings, drawings, and poetry. This teacher's writing is equally pertinent and ranges from topics such as the disgrace of closed school libraries, how the painter Degas was linked to music, and using technology as a teaching tool.

http://doyle-scienceteach.blogspot.com is a blog from a science teacher who focuses on teaching practices within his subject matter as well as his opinions and reflections on education and the world we live in. Topics range from a school marching-band shirt that depicts evolution, to the water in charter schools, to how it all equates to the cycles of life and mortality. It is safe to say the voice of this blog is decidedly for adults.

www.facebook.com/ is a very well-known free site for social networking. In fact it is the most used social network, with MySpace coming in second. Registration is required in order to use Facebook. Users can very easily form accounts and create their own personal home page in order to send their friends messages and update personal profiles to keep those friends informed on their activities. A user's profile can be set to public or private in order to control who is able to associate with them. Since the site is now worldwide, it is organized into networks by city, workplace, school, and region. Key points of Facebook are the vast amount of groups that users can join according to their interests and the numbers of features available for users to interact with.

Among these is the ability to share photos, give status updates, virtually "poke" a friend in order to get their attention online, and write a message or leave an attachment on someone's "wall."

http://kathyschrock.net/blog/ is a blog by the educator Kathy Schrock. Her thoughts, ideas, and discoveries are geared toward the use of technology as an educative tool. She raises discussions about topics like utilizing Twitter and the use of Google in the classroom. Her writing voice is very informal and welcoming, with poignant observations on how students are using technologies socially (for example, sharing music earbuds while sitting next to each other). This blog is a great resource for seeking out information and conversations surrounding educational technology that is extremely smart yet not intimidating.

http://mrcoyle.edublogs.org is a blog from Gary Coyle's grade 8 Humanities class in New Delhi, India. The unique quality of this class blog is that it has links to student blogs as well. The whole-class blog hosts a question for discussion in accordance with what information was covered that week, while personal student blogs respond to specific posts.

www.myspace.com is another very well-known free social networking site. Its popularity comes in second next to Facebook, with its slogan being "A Place for Friends." The site's blogging features are the main concept that makes up this social networking tool. Each profile contains a blogging area with space for content, media, and emotion. Users simply create a home page with profile information such as "About Me," and "Who I'd like to meet." There is a place for other users to post comments, images to portray a user's mood (emoticons), and a section for other details about the user.

http://plethoratech.blogspot.com is a blog for educators about teaching and learning. The author fills it with thought-provoking ideas on the learning process, reminders that our goal as educators is to always strive for better understanding, and suggestions and Web links to accomplish all of this.

www.rebeccablood.net is a website from Rebecca Blood, who has been blogging on rebecca's pocket since 1999. Her blog is an interesting amalgamation of articles and links pertaining to things that interest her. Among her varied interests are sustainability, Web culture, and media literacy. Rebecca is a pioneer in the blog world and is known for authoring *The Weblog Handbook: Practical Advice on Creating and Maintaining Your Blog.*

http://edublogs.org/ is a blog-hosting tool designed specifically for teachers and classrooms. Created and maintained by teachers for teachers, Edublogs is an ideal starter service for educators who are hoping to learn how to blog with their classes. The site features extensive support forums, video tutorials, and helpful documentation to aid you in setting up a blog community in your classroom. One of the best aspects of this site is the blog-management features (i.e., editing and monitoring of all content and comments) for teachers. All aspects of the site are free, with each account receiving 20 MB of upload space. This can be extended to 5 GB through a donation to the site. A unique feature of Edublogs is the ability to import preexisting blogs from sites such as Blogger, TypePad, or LiveJournal to the Edublogs server. The reverse, exporting blogs from Edublogs to other hosting sites, is also possible.

www.ning.com enables the creation of social networks for a closed group of individuals. This makes it perfect as a classroom and administrative group tool. It basically operates as an organized online meeting space, discussion forum, and information sharing space for students and educators alike. Each Ning site features a customizable layout and provides a place for discussion forums, photo and video sharing, event notices and invitations, link posting, chat capabilities, document and note sharing, blog hosting, group creation, and member profiles. Privacy features allow the site to be made available to anyone or invited members only, and all aspects of the site are completely free. Additionally, each Ning site is assigned its own unique Web address at ___.ning.com. This makes the site very easy to find. Members must set up a Ning account and specific identity in order to access other groups hosted on the Ning network.

http://posterous.com/ is a blog-hosting tool that works from your e-mail account. Their tagline is, "If you can e-mail, you can blog with posterous." It's an easy way to create group blogs or update multiple blogs all at once. All that is required is a two-step setup process on posterous.com. After setup, posterous.com supplies a unique email address where all information is sent. Posterous.com then does the posting for you! The site supports photos, videos, music, and documents. All aspects of the site are free to use, with the downside being a lack of any privacy features.

www.scribd.com/ is the largest social publishing company in the world. Whether students need a place to host their original works or teachers need a tool to facilitate the sharing of original class documents, Scribd is a simple, well-designed platform to meet a classroom's document-sharing needs. All accounts on the site are not only free of charge, but merely browsing the site does not require a free membership and is greatly facilitated by the impeccably organized genre categories. It is worth noting that any document you upload to the site is available for the public to read.

www.tumblr.com is a very basic blog-hosting tool. Advertised as "the easiest way to blog," single-author blogs can be set up with only one click. All aspects and options, however bare-bones they may be, are entirely free. Though there are no layout options, very few opportunities to customize the design, and no way to add applications to the page, Tumblr makes a great starter tool for quick, media-centric posts. Perhaps the best feature of the site is the ability to create blogging communities by following the blogs of others. After choosing to follow other blogs, updates from each of them will show up in a central location, making the need to check a large number of individual blogs obsolete. No privacy options for Tumblr blogs currently exist.

www.twitter.com is a micro-blogging application that challenges users to share links, questions, and other pieces of information in 140 characters or less. A Twitter account can be used in conjunction with note-taking software such as www.evernote.com and www.jott.com. All Twitter accounts are free, and users can share information as privately or publicly as they wish, through the use of personal messaging features and privacy settings that can be applied to the entire account. Setup of the account is easy and no downloads are required. However, desktop applications can be downloaded to facilitate the ease with which you maintain the account by receiving and making updates. In addition to being a great link-sharing tool, Twitter can be used as a vital source of real-time information, since many news websites (i.e., CNN and the New York Times) have Twitter accounts that they update regularly with links and breaking news stories.

http://weblogg-ed.com/ is the website of educator Will Richardson, author of *Blogs, Wikis, Podcasts, and Other Powerful Web Tools for Classrooms*. It has a plethora of information on using wikis, weblogs, audiocasts, and RSS as well as a host of other technologies. He also has links to important conferences and videos. Worth noting is the site's information on creating a consent form for a specific project.

Wikis

http://budtheteacher.com/wiki/ is a very content-rich wiki by Bud, a technology integrator and blogger extraordinaire. This wiki is chock-full of resources and links to other educators' blogs and wikis. Although not fancy, this wiki reads like a laundry list of digital information and resources.

http://delicious.com/ is a link aggregator. Once the application is installed, it's easy to collect, organize, and share your links with the entire Web community. Delicious is ideal for collecting information for research projects or papers. A single Delicious account could be used by an entire group or classroom, to organize and store links in one central location. Alternatively, each member can have their own account to collect research independently, and share it publicly with others. All aspects of Delicious are free, with a quick setup and easy-to-use service. Many Web pages have link-aggregator service icons, making saving a link to your Delicious account incredibly easy. Additional applications for Web browsers are available for free download.

www.etherpad.com is a real-time collaborative editing tool that ensures consistency between everyone's screens by logging the changes in real-time. This account allows for the creation and editing of unlimited documents. Each document receives its own unique URL with editing privileges open for up to eight users by invitation only, and the URL of these documents can be distributed and shared with anyone who may wish to view it. The basic account is free to use, but with purchase of upgrades available in order to access certain security features. These premium editions offer more privacy and access to support, making them well worth it. Additionally, EtherPad's chat feature makes it ideal for group papers that need to be completed outside of classroom time.

http://learning2shanghai.wetpaint.com is a wiki titled, Welcome to Learning the Wiki Way, by the educator Jason Welker. This wiki does a thorough job of informing teachers on how to create and operate a wiki. It also has information on wiki workshops, and teacher conferences that include topics like how to make your wiki fun.

http://savedarfurnhs.wetpaint.com is a wiki created by the eighth grade at North Hampton School in New Hampshire, after an assembly generated student interest and compassion for the genocide in Darfur. The site is set up as a complete information hub on Darfur itself and on what the students are doing to raise awareness and money for the people of Darfur. It is a very passionate website that is not only a great example of a productive and educative wiki, but a resourceful way to get other educators interested in this vital subject matter. This wiki also contains a great navigation bar with headings: The Darfur Song, Petitions and Protests, How You Can Help, What We Have Done, What We Need to Do, and Recent Activity in Darfur.

www.jott.com is a note-taking tool that utilizes phone calls made to a toll-free number that are collected, stored, and transformed into text. The basic function of Jott is to take audio, turn it into text, and post it to the location of your choice (i.e., email, blog, twitter update, etc.). What can you do with this technology? You can create notes for yourself with only a mobile phone, make to-do lists, email or text using only your voice, and even record interviews for class projects complete with perfect transcripts of the conversation. Although all of this technology comes with a price, the service is free to try out for a week. With a free week's account, you will be given a toll-free number to call in your audio, and Jott will place a text version of your audio in the location of your choice (i.e., email or blog). After the free week, you can end your trial period or purchase a monthly account for as little as $3.95. Pay-as-you-go accounts are available as well for $6.95 per every five minutes of audio.

www.moodle.com is a Course Management System (CMS), also known as a Learning Management System (LMS) or a Virtual Learning Environment (VLE). It is a free Web application that educators can use to create effective online learning sites. You must download a software package, but all versions of the program are free. Moodle can be used as an alternative to Blackboard or even Ning as a central place to organize course documents and create online forums for your students.

http://mpolselli.wetpaint.com/?t=anon is the wiki for Mrs. Polselli's fifth-grade class that she has set up with the free "create a website" site: www .wetpaint.com/. She has set it up to be a wonderful resource for keeping parents informed of classroom activities and to get her students excited about the school year. She includes PowerPoints of the class schedule, syllabus, and other important announcements. She also posts any featured books, musicians, contests, and webquests that will be part of her curriculum for the upcoming year.

http://pbworks.com/ is a site that offers free wiki templates in order for you to easily create your own classroom, business, or personal wiki. More advanced featured templates are available at a fee. The templates are categorized according to what they may be used for, so there are legal, campus, and project editions depending on your goal. Another plus is that all cost packages are available with no charge on a thirty-day trial basis, and packages are priced moderately at $8.00 to $20.00 per month.

http://supportblogging.com/Links+to+School+Bloggers#toc6 is a site that, although about supporting blogging, is technically a wiki to be explored and contributed to. You can think of it as a "how-to" manual for blogging. It is a free, informative, and instructional website that promotes and encourages the practice of educational blogging. The site is very well organized, with a table of contents that includes alphabetical running lists of personal blogs, definitions and lengthy descriptions on educational blogging, blogging community resources, and instructions on how to contribute to the SupportBlogging! page.

http://victoriaaurorahistoryfairproject.wetpaint.com is a student-created wiki that focuses on women soldiers in the Civil and Revolutionary Wars. The wiki was originally created for a history fair project. It includes photos and profiles of women soldiers, and is written in a very peer-friendly way that would draw any student in.

www.wetpaint.com/ is a free-of-charge social networking and wiki-hosting service. Simply put, Wetpaint is a great website to go through in order to easily create your own URL, blog, wiki, or forum. The company targets users who may not be as technologically savvy as others but who want to create efficient and effective websites. Among its strong points are a three-step wiki creator, the option to have educational sites be free of any advertising, and simple site navigation that allows you to seek and join sites rather than make your own.

www.wiki.com is a tool for facilitating the sharing and construction of knowledge by a group of people. A wiki is a Web page that can be viewed and modified by multiple people. The only drawback to a wiki is that changes do not occur in real time. This means that updates to the information should not occur at the same time since each change must be saved before it shows up on the page. Wikis can be viewed and used by anyone on the Internet, making them ideal for creating an authentic purpose for research and writing. Private wikis are also available at no extra charge. All aspects of the wiki service are free and relatively easy to set up with the tutorials provided on the site.

www.wikipedia.org/ is a very specific and prominent wiki known as "The Free Encyclopedia that anyone can edit." This resource is a multilingual, content-based encyclopedia project. It is a collaboration by anonymous volunteer authors, meaning that anyone with Internet access can contribute, create, and alter an entry on Wikipedia. The main idea is that Wikipedia entries should not be based on new research, but rather founded on existing information. Information should be edited within the appropriate policies and standards of the Wikipedia site in order to maintain true, genuine, accurate, and beneficial information for all readers. Searching is as simple as typing in the name of what you are interested in learning about. A great feature is the additional notes, references, and external links that are included at the end of each article. These can ultimately become resources that lead you to explore your original topic in greater depth.

http://wikisineducation.wetpaint.com is a wiki tutorial site that is hosted through the free website www.wetpaint.com/. This wiki serves not only as a community to inform educators on using wikis, but also as a means to start your own educational wiki. It has a variety of wiki samples to explore, use as samples, and contribute to. The wiki categories include higher education, classroom, group project, teacher created, and student peers.

http://writersrock.wetpaint.com is a website for middle school teachers using the Teachers College Writers and Readers Workshop model. Their goal statement includes the wish to "support each other in our teaching practice by sharing resources, systems and management strategies. . . ." The wiki encourages users to share tips, and begin discussions about their teaching practices.

Digital Storytelling

http://epencil.edublogs.org is a sixth-grade writing workshop weblog called The Electronic Pencil. The site showcases students' digital stories by embedding them into a wonderful class blog. Posts are very conscious of student climate, with threads like "what worries you, or what excites you?" It includes fun links like art tools, comic sites, crazy dictionary, and current events.

www.evernote.com is a note organization application powered by recognition technology. Though it's easy to create an account, understanding how to utilize all of the amazing features of the application will take an investment of time. The idea is that one can use their Evernote account to tag and organize information one encounters every day. For example, if you find a sign during a field trip of a historical site and want to remember the information, you can take a picture of the sign and upload it to your Evernote account. Then, Evernote's text-recognition technology will convert the image of the sign into text. The basic account option is free and includes a limited number of useful Web pages, images, and other media per month, but purchased premium accounts are available with 500 MB. Evernote can be used for everything from to-do lists, Web page favorites, audio, images from a camera or computer, and documents. It is also possible to send information to your Evernote account via email or Twitter.

www.flickr.com/ is an image- and video-hosting website that has gained much popularity for its user-friendly ability to share personal photographs. The site describes its main goals to be "helping people make their photos and content accessible to the people most important to them," and "creating new ways of organizing photos and video." Use of Flickr's basic account is completely free, with additional features/packages such as high-quality video as something available to paid subscribers. The home page with sign-up is very easy to navigate in order to get anyone set up to share photos and video. A virtual instructional tour breaks the whole process down into eight steps, and the About Us page is worth reading not only for the information on its founders and features, but also for its fun and quirky delivery.

http://jasonohler.com is the website of Dr. Jason Ohler, who is an expert at the practice of digital storytelling and the author of *Digital Storytelling in the Classroom*. His site boasts the phrase "To live, learn, work and play in the Digital Age," and is laden with articles, resources, and keynote addresses about digital storytelling. Links not to miss (under the About tab) include Portfolio, At work with teachers, and Pictures of home.

www.slideshare.com is a presentation creation and hosting tool. No downloads are required, and all membership accounts are free and unlimited. Privacy settings are available if you'd like to use them. You can make your presentation online, or choose to upload previous presentations you have constructed with other software (i.e., PowerPoint, open office, or Apple Keynote) and share it easily with a unique Web address. In addition to supporting other software presentation formats, SlideShare can also host documents and spreadsheets for easy participation. SlideShare also makes it simple to sync audio files to your presentation, or even embed your presentation into another website (i.e., blog or classroom home page). It also allows you to search for presentations and documents others have uploaded or created, using their very accessible search feature.

www.storycenter.org/ is the website for The Center for Digital Storytelling, which is an international nonprofit organization based in Northern California. Their focus is on the concept of real-life people telling their stories in a digital format such as still pictures, written scripts, video, and music. Their mission statement includes the phrase, "We assist youth and adults around the world in using media tools to share, record, and value stories from their lives. . . ." In addition to digital stories archived on their site, and a list of resources for educators, they also host storytelling workshops across the United States and Canada. Their original digital storytelling workshop is the format used by most digital storytellers and educators. Their book can be found online at www .storycenter.org.cookbook.html.

www.teachertube.com is a community-based site created by teachers for sharing instructional videos. Since it is monitored for relevance, appropriateness, and usefulness much more rigorously than YouTube, this site is an excellent place for students to search for original videos. Teachers will also find it to be a useful and free website for locating relevant resources and videos for curricular content as well as professional development and Web 2.0 tutorials. Anyone can contribute to the website, making it an ideal venue for posting class project videos that other students may find helpful.

www.vimeo.com is a higher-video-quality alternative to YouTube. Like other video-sharing websites, Vimeo is a democratic community, allowing anyone to upload their original work. Vimeo lauds itself on being a respectful community of creative people who are passionate about sharing the videos they make. As such, the site ensures the highest viewing quality for the videos they host, and can even support HD quality. Like TeacherTube, Vimeo also holds high standards of quality, respect, and originality for the videos they allow on the site, making it an extremely student-friendly resource.

http://wisdomlostwisdomfound.wikispaces.com/introduction is a wiki that showcases students' digital stories based on oral histories of their local community members. The site is set up almost in a report form with an introduction and overview of the history project, guiding questions and activities, and the solution to fill in the blanks of generations past. It is a very thought-provoking and inspiring resource for social change.

www.280slides.com is a presentation creation tool. Like SlideShare, there's no software to download and all accounts and services are free. Unlike

SlideShare, 280 Slides has the unique feature of a built-in media-searching tool, making researching media resources quick and easy to accomplish while building your presentation. Creating a presentation is essentially as easy as surfing the Web since all editing and research are done from the same Web browser. Additionally, the autosave and recovery features are very practical, and work well. When you are finished, you can download it to PowerPoint with one click.

Additional Pertinent Resources

http://community.discoveryeducation.com/ is the website for The Discovery Educator Network. The site frequently hosts free virtual conferences for teachers as a way to share ideas about the utilization of Web 2.0 applications in the classroom. The Network also hosts personal blogs of innovative educators, and maintains an up-to-date list of Web resources for the classroom. All webinars, resources, and applications on the site are free. It is possible to access all of the resources on the website without signing up for a free Discovery Educator Network membership; however, a free membership is necessary to attend live webinars.

www.edutopia.org/ hosts a variety of blogs written by professional educators in addition to producing professional development webinars (available to members only) and videos. Much of the content on the site is dedicated to Web 2.0 tools in the public school classroom. The site also features a range of research articles, in addition to having a helpful search feature for all of the content displayed. All aspects of the site except the webinars are free, though it is possible to become a member and support the site voluntarily in exchange for a subscription to *Edutopia* magazine, and access to all professional development webinars.

www.eschoolnews.com/ is a free online educator newspaper that started solely as a monthly printed paper in 1998. Their tagline is "Technology News for Today's K–20 Educator," and articles focus on all aspects of education technology from new products, to the Internet, to specific case studies and breaking events in education technology. The site is wonderfully organized, with categories of breaking news, most popular, funding, technology, conferences, best practices, superintendent's center, eclassroom news, and site of the week. Again, the site offers free registration and important email updates if you choose that option. It is worth noting that you can also view eSchoolNews articles without registering, but if you decide to use it as a consistent resource, registration is more practical.

www.loc.gov/index.html is the website for The Library of Congress. It is the largest library in the world and the oldest federal institution in the United States. The site is a great resource for learning about literacy projects such as the American Folklife Center, the Center for the Book, and the Poet Laureate. It also has maps, recordings, and manuscripts. Although the actual library in Washington, D.C., is not open to public lending, the site itself can be explored for hours, and serves as a great way to promote research, reading, and many other projects within the classroom.

www.scholastic.com features a teacher resource page with a classroom home page builder. The home page builder is free and can even be hosted by scholastic.com for free. Though it's easy to create a home page in three steps using the builder, Scholastic also has a tutorial for this to aid you in the process. The security options for the free home pages are excellent, and Scholastic ensures that the student version is advertisement free. Additionally, the teacher resource page features a discussion forum for teachers to share their own innovative ideas.

http://teenink.com/ is a monthly print magazine, book series, and website that was founded in 1989 and is completely dependent on teen submissions. It is marketed to and published by teenagers from the nonprofit organization The Young Author's Foundation. The main purpose of the magazine is to foster the development of teens' writing, reading, and critical thinking skills while giving them their own venue to do so. The magazine publishes anthologies, perpetually accepts writing submissions, and has a large focus on poetry. The website is very creative and easy to navigate, with categories such as poetry, fiction, nonfiction, hot topics, opinion, art and photos, and reviews. They also host many contests not only for writing, but magazine artwork as well. Both the site and the magazine are free and widely distributed in classrooms nationwide with a simple online request. It is worth noting that there is always the option of a donation since they are maintaining themselves on a not-for-profit basis.

Bibliography

Alvermann, Donna E. 2001. "Effective Literacy Instruction for Adolescents." Executive Summary and Paper Commissioned by the National Reading Conference, Chicago, Illinois. Updated version October 30.

Atwell, Nancie. 1998. *In the Middle, New Understandings About Writing, Reading, and Learning,* 2d ed. Portsmouth, NH: Boynton/Cook.

Biancarosa, Gina, and Catherine E. Snow. 2006. "Reading Next: A Vision for Action and Research in Middle and High School Literacy." 2d ed. In *A Report to Carnegie Corporation of New York.* Washington, DC: Alliance for Excellent Education.

Black, Rebecca W. 2006. "Language, Culture and Identity in Fanfiction." *eLearning* 3 (2). Available at www.wwwords.co.uk/pdf/freetoview.asp?j=elea&vol=3&issue=2&year=2006&article=5_Black_ELEA_3_2_web.

———. 2005. "Access and Affiliation: The Literacy and Composition Practices of English Language Learners." *Journal of Adolescent and Adult Literacy* 49 (2): 118–28.

Blood, Rebecca. 2002. *The Weblog Handbook: Practical Advice on Creating and Maintaining Your Blog.* New York: Basic Books.

Chesney, Thomas. 2006. "An Empirical Examination of Wikipedia's Credibility." *First Monday* 11 (11). Available at http://firstmonday.org/htbin/cgiwrap/bin/ojs/index.php/fm/article/viewArticle/1413/(http://en.wikipedia.org/wiki/Wikipedia:Overview_FAQ.

Cohen, Noam. 2009. "Twitter on the Barricades: Six Lessons Learned." *New York Times,* June 20. Available at www.nytimes.com/2009/06/21/weekinreview/21cohenweb.html?scp=1&sq=twitter%20iran%20june%202009&st=cse.

Crystal, David. 2008. *Txting: The Gr8 Db8*. New York: Oxford University Press.

eSchoolNews Staff and Wire Service Reports. 2008. "Blogging Helps Encourage Teen Writing." *ESchoolNews*, April 30. Available at www.eschoolnews.com/news/top-news/?i=53663.

Frey, Nancy, and Douglas Fisher. 2008. *Teaching Visual Literacy: Using Comic Books, Graphic Novels, Anime, Cartoons, and More to Develop Comprehension and Thinking Skills*. Thousand Oaks, CA: Corwin Press.

Funk, Jeanne, Heidi Baldacci, Tracie Pasold, and Jennifer Baumgardner. 2004. "Violence Exposure in Real-Life, Video Games, Television, Movies, and the Internet: Is There Desensitization?" *Journal of Adolescence* 27 (1): 23–39.

Gee, James Paul. 2007. *What Video Games Have to Teach Us About Learning and Literacy*. 2d ed. Revised and updated. Hampshire, UK: Palgrave Macmillan.

———. 1996. *Social Linguistics and Literacies: Ideology in Discourses*. Florence, KY: Routledge.

Hart, Peter D., Research Associates/Public Opinion Strategies. 2005. "Are College Graduates Prepared for College and Work?" *Achieve, Inc.* Available at www.achieve.org/RisingtotheChallenge.

Howe, Neil, and William Strauss. 2000. *Millennials Rising: The Next Great Generation*. New York: Vintage.

Ito, Mizuko, Heather A. Horst, Matteo Bittanti, Danah Boyd, Becky Herr-Stephenson, Patricia G. Lange, C. J. Pascoe, and Laura Robinson. 2008. "Living and Learning with New Media: Summary of Findings from the Digital Youth Project." *The John D. and Catherine T. MacArthur Foundation Reports on Digital Media and Learning*. Available at http://digitalyouth.ischool.berkeley.edu/report.

Lankshear, Colin, and Michelle Knobel. 2006. *New Literacies: Everyday Practices and Classroom Learning*. Columbus, OH: Open University Press.

Lenhart, Amanda, Arafeh Sousan, Aaron Smith, and Alexandra Rankin Macgill. 2008. "Writing, Technology, and Teens." Pew Internet & American Life Project. April 24. Available at www.pewinternet.org/.

Lenhart, Amanda, and Mary Madden. 2007. "Social Networking Websites and Teens: Teens, Privacy, and Online Social Networks." Pew Internet & American Life Project. January 3. Available at www.pewinternet.org/.

Lenhart, Amanda, Mary Madden, Alexandra Rankin Macgill, and Aaron Smith. 2007. "Teens and Social Media: The Use of Social Media Gains a Greater Foothold in Teen Life as They Embrace the Conversational Nature of Interactive Online Media." Pew Internet & American Life Project. December 19. Available at www.pewinternet.org/.

Lenhart, Amanda, Mary Madden, and Paul Hitlin. 2005. "Teens and Technology: Youth Are Leading the Transition to a Fully Wired and Mobile Nation." *Pew Internet & American Life Project.* July 27. Available at www.pewinternet.org/.

Lessig, Lawrence. 2008. *Remix: Making Art and Commerce Thrive in the Hybrid Economy.* New York: Penguin.

Myracle, Lauren. 2005. *ttyl (Talk to You Later—Internet Girls).* New York: Harry N. Abrams.

Ohler, Jason. 2007. *Digital Storytelling in the Classroom: New Media Pathways to Literacy, Learning, and Creativity.* Thousand Oaks, CA: Corwin Press.

Palfrey, John, and Urs Gasser. 2008. *Born Digital: Understanding the First Generation of Digital Natives.* New York: Basic Books.

Persky, Hillary R., Mary C. Daane, and Ying Jin. 2003. "The Nation's Report Card, Writing: 2002." *National Center for Education Statistics.* Available at http://nces.ed.gov/.

Prensky, Marc. 2001. "Digital Natives, Digital Immigrants." *On the Horizon* 9 (5).

Richardson, Will. 2006. *Blogs, Wikis, Podcasts, and Other Powerful Tools for the Classroom.* Thousand Oaks, CA: Corwin.

Rutenberg, Jim. 2004. "Web Offers Hefty Voice to Critics of Mainstream Journalists." *New York Times,* October 28. Available at www.nytimes.com/2004/10/28/politics/campaign/28blog.html?scp=9&sq=blogs+dan+rather+&st=nyt.

Street, Brian V. 1993. *Cross-Cultural Approaches to Literacy (Cambridge Studies in Oral and Literate Culture).* Cambridge, UK: Cambridge University Press.

Tapscott, Don, and Anthony D. Williams. 2006. *Wikinomics: How Mass Collaboration Changes Everything.* New York: Penguin.

Tugend, Alina. 2008. "Multitasking Can Make You Lose . . . Um . . . Focus. . . ." *New York Times,* October 24. Available at www.nytimes.com/2008/10/25/business/yourmoney/25shortcuts.html?ref=weekinreview.

Vandewater, Elizabeth, Mi-suk Shim, and Allison Caplovitz. 2004. "Linking Obesity and Activity Level with Children's Television and Video Game Use." *Journal of Adolescence* 27 (1): 71–85.

"What Content-Area Teachers Should Know About Adolescent Literacy." 2007. National Institute for Literacy report. Available at www.nifl.gov/publications/publications.html.

"Writing: A Ticket to Work . . . Or a Ticket Out. A Survey of Business Leaders." 2004. Report of The National Commission on Writing for America's Families, Schools, and Colleges. September. Available at www.writingcommission.org/prod_downloads/writingcom/writing-ticket-to-work.pdf.

Index

Harry Potter, 14, 28, 60, 107
Heath, Shirley B., 21
Hosseini, Khaled (*Kite Runner, The*), 53
Howe, Neil (*Millennials Rising*), xii, 8
How to Help Save Darfur wiki, 57
Huffington Post, 46

IAYF (Information at Your Fingertips), 31
identity
    creating sense of, 96–97
    in literacy instruction, 84–85
iMovie, 75
inquiry in literacy instruction, 85–87
instant messaging
    characteristics of, 27–28
    as new literacy, 22–23
Instant Messenger, xi–xii, 9
interest in literacy instruction, 85–87
Internet. *See also* World Wide Web
    defined, 31
    Millennials' use of, 9
issues in literacy instruction
    authenticity, 80–82
    cognitive development, 87–88
    community, 88–90
    interest and inquiry, 85–87
    meaning and identity, 84–85
    motivation, 92
    practice, 82–83
    process, 90–92
    relevance, 83–84
    safety, 78–80
Ito, Mizuko ("Living and Learning with
    New Media"), 8

journaling, 51

Kathy Schrock's Kaffeeklatsch blog, 48
Kite Runner, The (Hosseini), 50, 53
Knobel, Michelle (*New Literacies*), 38

Lankshear, Colin (*New Literacies*), 38
learning
    with digital technology, 12–15
    digital technology with, 12–13
Lessig, Lawrence (*Remix*), 15

Library of Congress, 73
linking blogs, 45–46
literacy
    defined, 21–22
    low-achievement by students,
        research on, 7–8
    problems with teaching, 15
    in students' lives today, 4–8
literacy instruction
    digital technologies in, 12–15
    issues in (*see* issues in literacy
        instruction)
    learning, being, connecting in, 12–15
    new literacies to support (*see* new
        literacies)
    problems with, 15
literature, value of knowing, 41–42
LiveJournal virtual community
    blogging, 51
    Millennials' use of, 8
"Living and Learning with New Media"
    (Ito, et al.), 8

MacArthur Digital Youth Project, 18
MacArthur Foundation, 8
Mama Day (Naylor), 30
Maniac Magee (Spinelli), 56
meaning in literacy instruction, 84–85
Meyer, Stephanie (*Twilight*), 107
micro-blogging, 98–101
Microsoft, 31
Microsoft Word, 81
Millennial generation, xii
Millennials, characteristics of, 8–11
Millennials Rising (Howe and Strauss),
    xii, 8
mobile tools, literacy through, 104–105
Monk Kidd, Sue (*Secret Life of Bees, The*),
    68–69
Mortenson, Greg (*Three Cups of Tea*), 86
motivation in literacy instruction, 92
MovieMaker, 75, 76
multimodal texts, 32–33
multitasking, 9, 10
"Multitasking Can Make You Lose . . .
    Um . . . Focus . . ." (Tugend), 10

virtual, three-dimensional worlds, as new literacy, 29–30
visual literacy, as new literacy, 36–38

Wagner, Mark, 100
Web. *See* World Wide Web
Web 1.0, 31
Web 1.0 before Web 2.0, 94
Web 2.0, xi, 31–32
Webkinz online virtual world, 103
Weblogg-Ed, 63–64
Weblog Handbook, The (Blood), 45
weblogs. *See* blogs
Welcome to Learning the Wiki Way wiki, 57
Welker, Jason, 57
What Video Games Have to Teach Us About Learning and Literacy (Gee), 22, 101, 102
Wikinomics (Tapscott and Williams), 70
Wikipedia, 9, 54, 70
wikis
    compared to blogs, 70–71
    creation of, 44–45
    defined, xi, 54
    functioning of, 54–58
    historical overview, 55–56
    as new literacy, 38–41
    research with, 56–57
    resources, online, 118–22
    setup and use, 71–73
    value of, xii, 18, 54–55
Wikis in Education, 55, 72
Wikispaces, 72
Williams, Anthony D. (*Wikinomics*), 70
Wisdom Lost, Wisdom Found wiki, 60
Witnessing History project, 109
Wizard Writer's blog, 49

Word of the Year, 46
workshop model, 3–4, 16–17
World Wide Web
    changes in, 31–34
    information gathering on, 12–13
    Millennials' use of, 8
writing
    changing nature of, xi–xii
    digital technology in, 12–15
    importance of, 11–12
    low-achievement by students, research on, 7–8
    new technologies for (*see* new literacies)
    topic selection, 40
writing instruction
    integrating technology into, 40–41
    issues in (*see* issues in literacy instruction)
    literacy in students' lives today, 4–8
    Millennials in, characteristics of, 8–11
    new literacies to support (*see* new literacies)
    new technologies for (*see* new literacies)
    problems with, 15
    students, examples of typical, 1–2, 4–7
    today, 2–19
    workshop model, 3–4
writing workshop, 16–17
    topic selection in, 40

Yang, Gene L. (*American-Born Chinese*), 103
YouTube website
    digital stories in, 60
    as new literacy, 23–24, 25